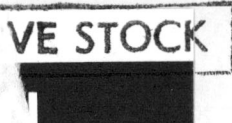

THE BEGINNERS GUIDE TO SHOTOKAN KARATE

GICHIN FUNAKOSHI
The father of modern day karate, who was a scholar of the Chinese classics as well as a karate master, was born in Shuri, Okinawa Prefecture, in 1868 and died in Tokyo in 1957.

The Beginners Guide
to
SHOTOKAN
KARATE

by
John van Weenen
6th Dan

Chief Instructor:
Traditional Association of Shotokan Karate

First published November 1983
First Reprint April 1984
Second Reprint October 1985
Third Reprint August 1986
Fourth Reprint May 1987
Fifth Reprint January 1988
Sixth Reprint April 1989
Seventh Reprint December 1990
Eighth Reprint July 1991
Ninth Reprint July 1992
Tenth Reprint July 1993
Eleventh Reprint April 1995

The author would like to thank the following
instructors for their assistance:
Christopher Burton 4th Dan
Jane van Weenen 4th Dan
Gursharan Sahota 4th Dan
Bernard Coppen 4th Dan
Andy Kidby 4th Dan
Roy Hazelwood 4th Dan
John Caves 3rd Dan
Michael Batten 3rd Dan
Donovan Slue 3rd Dan
Leslie Albone 3rd Dan
"Mac" Roome 3rd Dan
Azad Kumar 3rd Dan
Alan Bristow 3rd Dan
Also Mrs Irene Leslie for her much appreciated help with the fourth edition and Joanne Shenton, the
General Manager of the Lingfield Health Club, Kimbolton Road, Bedford, for the use of her premises for
the Weight Training Sequence.

ISBN NO 0 9517660 2 3
© Copyright 1983 John van Weenen

Published by John van Weenen, Fineshade Abbey, Fineshade, Northants NN17 3BB
Distributed by Biblios Publishers' Distribution Services Ltd, Star Road, Partridge Green, West Sussex
RH13 8LD. Telephone 01403 710971. Facsimile 01403 711143
Distributors to the Martial Arts Trade:
Blitz Corporation Ltd, 112 Bellegrove Road, Welling, Kent DA16 3QD.
Telephone 0181 303 2276. Facsimile 0181 303 8850
Shogun International, 87 Gayford Road, London W12 9BY. Telephone 0181 749 2022.
Facsmile 0181 740 1086
Printed by White Crescent Press Ltd, Crescent Road, Luton LU2 0AG

I dedicate this book to my wife Jane...

... and to my teacher Kanazawa Sensei

In the Dojo in 1969 – Sensei and student

CONTENTS

PREFACE

The reasons that led me to write this book are many. However, the overriding and deciding factor was the beginner's need for an elementary instruction manual that covered the three basic aspects of karate training, written by a westerner for westerners.

The majority of books on the market today have been written by Japanese, and quite rightly so, for in my opinion they are better qualified to write and teach Karate-Do than any other people. Having said that, in my experience over the last 20 years, many books have tended to be a little overpowering for the average beginner. Consequently, he learns very little from them.

I hope "The Beginner's Guide to Shotokan Karate" will rectify this. It is intended as a manual to assist club training and to enable the beginner to follow the basic fundamentals that he has been taught by his own teacher. Of course technique will differ from instructor to instructor, each having his own "Body System", but by and large Shotokan is universal in its basic concepts, and the reader should bear this in mind when comparing techniques.

As a traditionalist, I feel some measure of responsibility in the continuance of Karate-Do as a way of life, not merely as a sport, for I feel if the art has survived since the sixth century, it *must* be good and have a great deal to offer, otherwise it would have disappeared a long time ago.

May I take this opportunity of thanking Mr Alan Cooke who so painstakingly took the many photographs and without whose help this book would not have been possible.

John van Weenen
November 1983

1

A BEGINNERS VIEW

I came to Karate by chance. Oh I had from time to time observed groups of exponents in various positions of self-defence, and my son was a keen participant, but it never occurred to me that here was an activity with which I would become involved, let alone enthralled by. As a lapsed sportsman of approaching middle years, it was the organised keep fit that first attracted me — the twenty-minute warm-up period that, under the guidance of trained experts, systematically and scientifically stretched and toned up all the muscles and sinews of the body.

I soon discovered, almost without realising the fact, that I had entered into the spirit of Karate, and having come to terms with the early movements, I became aware of a re-awakening of a forgotten boyhood emotion — anticipation. As I looked forward to each new lesson, I would practise at home in front of the bathroom mirror. It was at this stage, however, that I became a little frustrated. My problems, in common with others no doubt, were two-fold. Firstly in remembering the sequence of previously taught movements, and secondly, being a less than gifted linguist, in grasping the Japanese commands and terminology. As a consequence I was forever Gyaku-tzuki-ing when I should have been Mae-geri-ing.

My disappointment was in being unable to find any suitable publication, aimed at the beginner, that supplemented the lessons of the Dojo, was written in basic Western terms, explained simply and pictorially the movements, and served as a quick yet comprehensive guide. Life, however, is very much about being in the right place at the right time. For me to have come to the sport under the guidance of Sensei van Weenen was indeed a stroke of good fortune, and when he asked me to assist him in producing such a book, aimed primarily for the benefit of the beginner, I was naturally delighted.

My observation is that Karate brings untold benefits to its fortunate exponents — confidence, physical fitness, self-defence, and so much more. By its very teachings it instils the virtues of honour and consideration, encouraging always a greater awareness of one's fellow creatures, and a genuine desire to leave only pleasant and fond memories as one journeys along "The Way".

If this book assists in achieving any of these objectives it will have provided a worthwhile service to the individual, and have been of benefit to Karate Do.

Left: In the Dojo — Sensei and student.   Paul Hooley, 1983.

FOREWORD

John van Weenen is well suited to author this book on Shotokan Karate, having trained for twenty years with the great names of the style. John is one of the few Westerners who can appreciate that there is more to Karate than the purely physical. The very use he makes of the word "Traditional" in the title of his own association confirms that he is devoted to the deeper aspects of this fascinating art. It is so very important, when learning Karate, to understand that it is more than just an impressive physical system; it is a deep philosophy and a unique expression of the Japanese warrior spirit. To teach the techniques without the underlying meaning and significance is only to graze the surface.

I well remember my teachers patiently explaining the importance of attitude to training; the need to train and constantly return to basics. It is only by constantly practising the basic techniques of Karate that the student can learn to react instinctively. The proper practice of Karate – as described in John's excellent book – leaves the mind calm and relaxed. It becomes cleared of the clutter of preconceptions and "when to do what". Having reached this stage, the person is truly competent.

I see so many Karate students today who believe that success in competition is the be all and end all of Karate. To be sure, the sporting aspect is healthy and enjoyable, but it is not the major part of Karate. The original idea behind Karate was not to win competitions; not even to be effective in self-defence (though Karate certainly produces this effectively), but to develop the character and mind of the student. The true Karateka is, unfortunately, a rare beast in this day and age. We have embraced the actions but not the philosophy. John van Weenen is a true Karateka and, consequently, his work is all the more important to those who are following the "Way". It is not just another manual; it is a well written, concise insight into Shotokan Karate – a major school of Japanese Karate.

David Mitchell

Secretary Martial Arts Commission.
Secretary British Karate Federation.
Secretary of English Karate Council.
Member of Directing Committee of European Karate Union.
Member of Directing Committee of World Union of Karate Organisations.

November 1983

KARATE
YESTERDAY AND TODAY

Present day Karate can be traced directly back to the time of Daruma, the Founder of Zen Buddhism. About 1400 years ago, he left Western India on foot for China to give lectures on Buddhism.

His journey of several thousand miles was perilous to say the least, for he had to cross the Himalayas, unbridged rivers, as well as vast stretches of wilderness. He made his journey alone, which gives us a clue to his spiritual as well as physical strength.

In later years, Daruma introduced to his many followers a system of physical movements to improve their strength, following a journey to the Shao-Lin Temple when most of them fell by the way-side from exhaustion.

With this system the Monks of the Shao-Lin Temple came to be known throughout China for their courage and fortitude.

In later times it came to be known as Shorin-Ji Kempo, and this method eventually reached the Ryukyu Islands and developed into Okinawa-Te, the forerunner of present day Karate.

The two Okinawan Masters, Azato and Itosu, were most responsible for teaching and influencing Funakoshi – the father of modern day Karate.

Karate was first introduced to the Japanese public in 1922, when Funakoshi, who was then Professor at the Okinawa Teacher's College, was invited to lecture and demonstrate at an exhibition of Traditional Martial Arts sponsored by the Ministry of Education. His demonstration so impressed the audience that he was flooded with requests to teach in Tokyo.

Instead of returning to Okinawa, Funakoshi taught Karate at various universities, and in 1936 established the Shotokan, a great landmark in the history of Karate in Japan.

In 1955 the Japan Karate Association came into being with Funakoshi as its chief instructor.

Over the years, many of Funakoshi's students have become teachers and masters in their own right, so we see the formation of various styles of Karate, each group basically following Funakoshi's teachings, with its leader developing his own style and technique in accordance with his own "Body System".

Karate has spread to almost every country in the civilised world. It is gaining in popularity everywhere, not only as a Martial Art and Self Defence, but also as a competitive sport.

The latter worries me, for I cannot help feeling that when the J.K.A. arranged and held the first All Japan Karate Championships in 1957, thus putting sport Karate on the map, they had unwittingly grasped the (Shotokan) Tiger by its tail!

INTRODUCTION
BASIC TECHNIQUES

The fundamental techniques of Karate are punching, striking, blocking and kicking, and certain considerations need to be observed before they can be performed effectively.

The following factors should be taken into account:

Form – Balance – Centre of Gravity.
Concentration of Power.
Rhythm.
Timing.
Hara – Hips.

Form: Correct form is very important in the execution of Karate techniques as the body must harmonize in order to acquire the stability necessary to sustain the shock of delivering a kick or punch.

Balance: Good balance is essential when performing any Karate technique, especially kicks. At times the body's whole weight must be supported on one leg or transferred quickly from one leg to the other.

Centre of Gravity: Involves Hara, the body's physical and spiritual centre of gravity. Any technique no matter what direction must keep the Hara at a constant level. For example whilst performing Oi Zuki, if at the halfway stage the legs are straightened causing the Hara to rise, and then lowered as the punch is completed, the full power of the technique will not be propelled in a forward direction (towards the opponent).

Concentration of Power: When performing basic techniques the body should remain relaxed and only tensed at the end of the movement when contact is made. This tension is known as "Kime" or focus. Physics dictate that a muscle that is contracted cannot move as quickly as one that is relaxed. Both muscles and tendons should be kept relaxed to allow instant response to changing circumstances. "Kime" is often misunderstood as being "Tensing". "Kime" is relaxing, tensing at the appropriate time and then relaxing.

Rhythm: Is essential in most sports. Think of the poetry of the hurdler or perhaps the butterfly swimmer for example.

In Karate, rhythm is more noticeable in "Kata" and some Karateka have better rhythm than others. Ultimately, a person's "Kinetic" sense is responsible for a Kata being good – or very good.

Rhythm keeps each technique in Kata separate, yet joins them harmoniously together as a whole.

Timing: Good timing is vital and if incorrect, will cause the technique to fail. A punch delivered too soon may be out of range and therefore rendered ineffective, whilst a punch delivered too late may result in no uncertain terms for the executor.

Hara: All body power should emanate from the Hara, the body's natural centre of gravity. If tension is only applied to the muscles of the forearm when punching, the punch will be weak, using only a fraction of the body's capability. Understanding the Hara is the single most important factor in the execution of Karate techniques, for without this knowledge the student will progress up to a point – and no further.

Hips: Coupled with Hara is the Hip movement or "Tanden". When performing basic techniques, the hips should rotate rather than undulate. Of course there are exceptions to this rule, as with some kicks, but by and large, the mechanics of the hip movement must be appreciated and the laws of action and reaction understood. The timing of the hips is crucial to the success of the technique.

PREVENTION OF LONG-TERM INJURY TO JOINTS

Prior to A.D. 1900, Karate development was a slow, gradual process which had spanned centuries. This all changed with the research and teachings of **Funakoshi Sensei** and the acceptance of Karate in Japan following his demonstration in Kyoto in 1915.

With the exception of several hundred American G.I.s after World War II had finished, virtually all the students of Karate between 1915 and 1960 were Oriental – more accurately, they were Japanese. The fact that they were shorter and more squat than their Western counterparts resulted in a difference in the mechanics of the techniques of punching, kicking, striking and blocking. This difference was not **understood immediately** by the Japanese instructors who brought Karate to the West.

Consequently, the long-limbed Westerners allowed their punches and kicks to terminate only when the arm or leg would not travel any further. Of course, we now know that "locking out" a punch or kick will aggravate the joint; so much so, that eventually it will become arthritic. The arm or leg must be stopped just short of its maximum travel by **utilising the appropriate muscles** to focus or "kime".

At present, there is no known cure for osteoarthritis, which affects the joints of many elderly people. Regular exercise through Karate training will help combat this affliction. Incorrect Karate training may hasten its approach. This point cannot be made too strongly.

KATA

Kata are the formal exercises of classical Karate. They are formulated in geometrical patterns and consist of various sequences of physical techniques, both defensive and offensive, against imaginary opponents. All **Kata** begin and end on the same spot and all are preceeded and concluded with a bow (Rei).

Traditional **Kata** are the means by which the ancient Karate practitioners have transmitted their knowledge down through the generations to the present day. Karate-do owes much to the practice of **Kata** for its very existence.

By learning **Kata**, students of Karate **"Walk in the Footsteps"** of the greatest Karate exponents that have ever lived. Furthermore, if the **Kata** are performed with confidence and humility, in time, the student may even be able to **sense the thoughts** of those who created them.

All **Kata** originated in **China**, although some have been developed from their original forms.

From a physical development point of view, there are two main aims. The first is **the strengthening of bone and muscle** to maximise the efficiency of one's biomechanics. The second aim is to **develop fast reflexes** and movements, increasing the ability to respond quickly to a self defence situation.

There are also non-physical benefits to be gained from constant practice through the integration of **mind, body and spirit**. Courtesy is developed through the practice of **Rei** and **Awareness** (Zanshin) is heightened.

Every movement has function and meaning, there being **no superfluous** actions whatsoever.

Correct breathing is vital, and **Kiai** serves to intensify the power of the technique upon execution.

About **50 Kata** have come down to us to the present day, and it's probably true to say that **Funakoshi Sensei** did more to systemise them than any other person.

Of the many advantages **Kata** undoubtedly has, it also allows one to **practice alone**, anywhere and without **special equipment** of any kind. All Karate **Kata** begin and end with a defensive technique, a fact reiterated by the famous saying of Gichin Funakoshi **"There is no first attack in Karate-do"**.

KUMITE

Kumite (Sparring) is the training method whereby the practical application of the techniques of defense and attack can be put to the test.

The advantage of training with a partner as opposed to oneself allows the participants to develop strong attacks and powerful blocks, whilst at the same time improving ones **Kime** (Focus), **Accuracy, Timing** and **Maai** (Distancing).

Kumite is a relatively modern innovation, having its beginnings in the early 1900's, being developed by **Funakoshi Sensei** and later by **Nakayama Sensei** in their respective positions as Chief Instructors to the **Japan Karate Association** (J.K.A.)

The practice of **Kumite** in its ultimate form, **Jiyū Kumite** (Free Sparring) is the closest assimilation to real combat possible, but requires perfect control on the part of both contestants.

A great deal of research has gone into **Kumite** training by the J.K.A., culminating in 1957 with the first **All Japan Karate Championships,** an event that continues right up to the present day, and is immensely popular.

Kumite training, therefore, should follow a set pattern, proven over the years along the following lines:

GOHON KUMITE	– Five Attack Sparring
SAMBON KUMITE	– Three Attack Sparring
KIHON IPPON KUMITE	– Basic One Attack Sparring
KAESHI IPPON KUMITE	– Basic One Attack with Stepping Counter
JIYŪ IPPON KUMITE	– Semi-Free One Attack Sparring
OKURI JIYŪ IPPON KUMITE	– Semi-Free Two Attack Sparring (1st attack Designated – 2nd Free)
JIYŪ KUMITE	– Free Sparring

Gohon Kumite teaches the proficiency of formal techniques, whilst **Sambon Kumite** teaches the same, but with the addition of multi-level attacks. In **Kihon Ippon Kumite** the emphasis is placed on being able to block one very strong attack and counter instantaneously. In my opinion, this form of Kumite is probably the most important, as it develops the students ability to **Kime** (focus).

By **relaxing, tensing** and **relaxing** again, the correct muscles needed for the execution of the technique are utilised and contracted at the right moment, thus aiding muscular development considerably. It also teaches **Maai** (distancing), a most essential factor, together with **timing,** enabling the block and counter attack to be left to the very last moment.

Jiyū Ippon Kumite is the transistional stage between **Kihon Ippon Kumite** and **Jiyū Kumite.** It builds on timing and distancing and encourages a more **fluid** and less informal approach. Combination techniques play a bigger part as does **Tai Sabaki** (Body Shifting).

PART 1 KIHON
BASIC TECHNIQUES

The following 84 pages deal exclusively with the more popular Basic Techniques of **Punching, Striking, Blocking and Kicking**. All of these techniques can be performed in one or other of the basic Shotokan stances. As this book is intended for **Beginners up to Black Belt** (Shodan), only the following stances need be mastered. Having said that, students should train hard and endeavour to develop strong stances, as they are primarily the basis for techniques to come.

 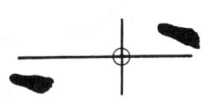

ZENKUTSU DACHI – FRONT STANCE
A strong attacking stance with 70% of the body weight over the front leg. Feet are approximately 4ft. to 4ft. 6ins. apart and are hip width wide.

 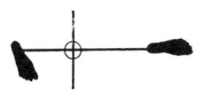

KŌKUTSU DACHI – BACK STANCE
Used mainly for blocking frontal attacks, having 70% of the body weight over the back leg. The front foot is directly in line with the heel of the back foot and they are 4ft. to 4ft. 6ins. apart.

KIBA DACHI – STRADDLE LEG STANCE
Very effective when used in conjunction with Side Snap or Thrust Kicks. Body weight is spread evenly between both legs and the feet are twice shoulder width apart. Feet should be turned in slightly and knees pushed out.

 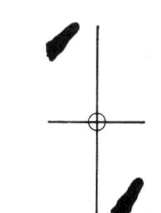

FUDO DACHI – ROOTED STANCE
A very strong stance midway between Zenkutsu and Kiba Dachi. The body weight is slightly more forward than back. Both feet are at a 45° angle and are twice shoulder width apart, being hip width apart when viewed from the the front.

NEKO ASHI – DACHI – CAT STANCE
A beautiful stance mainly used when blocking. With 90% of the body weight over the back leg, this stance is ideal for kicking with the front leg. The heel of the front foot remains off the floor.

 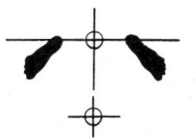

HACHIJI DACHI –
NATURAL OPEN LEG STANCE
The Natural Open Leg Stance is assumed after bowing and on the command of "yoi". The feet are hip width apart.

INDICATES
CENTRE OF GRAVITY

PUNCHING

Theoretical Considerations for Punching

In basic training, most punches start from the hip but once they have been perfected it may be necessary to punch from any position. Karate punches, in the main, travel in a straight line – the shortest distance between two points – and in an ideal situation, the opposite arm should do the same, in a reverse direction of course. Twisting the wrist on contact aids focus and exhalation. The timing of the beginning of a punch is crucial. If the fist leaves the waist too soon, it will have a pushing effect into its target and be only as strong as the weight or momentum of the person punching allows. Correspondingly, should the punch leave the hip too late, it will never gather momentum in time for it to have any appreciable effect.

Class performing Stepping Punch – during outdoor training session

13

CHOKU ZUKI
STRAIGHT PUNCH

Choku Zuki is the most basic Karate punch and is learned in the Hachiji Dachi stance. The punching hand begins at the waist in the inverted position and travels in a straight line to the target. It stays relaxed, as does the rest of the body until just prior to the end of its travel, when it twists 180° and the whole body is tensed. The opposite arm moves in harmony with the punching arm but of course in the reverse direction. Contact is made with Seiken (Fore Fist).

Application

1

2

3

4

15

OI ZUKI
STEPPING PUNCH

Application

Oi Zuki is virtually the same as Choku Zuki but performed whilst stepping forward or back. Starting from the Gedan Barai position bring the rear leg up to the front leg, keeping them both bent at this point, and then carry on forward into the next Zenkutsu Dachi. The arms remain in almost the same position right until the end of the technique and then exchange places, thus utilising fully the snapping action of the arms. At this point, the hips should be square on, body tensed and breath exhaled.

1

2

3

4

GYAKU ZUKI
REVERSE PUNCH

Application

Gyaku Zuki is a technique, usually performed on the spot, using the reverse hand to deliver the punch. It is possibly Karate's strongest punch, relying very much on applying the power generated by twisting the hips. From the Yoi position in Zenkutsu Dachi with the left hand open, commence the punch and the withdrawal of the left arm simultaneously. As in the photographs opposite it is important to keep the hips still in the 45° position as well as the body (Hanmi) until the second half of the technique.

As the right hand turns over to punch so the left inverts and at this point the right hip is thrust forward to the maximum. The breath is exhaled and the body tensed.

The final action of the hands, arms, hips, body, breathing and tension must culminate simultaneously.

1

2

3

4

MOROTE ZUKI
DOUBLE PUNCH (AUGMENTED)

Application

Morote Zuki begins by having both hands inverted on their respective hips, and in this technique, both arms punch together. Either or both fists make contact – one punching, both punching, or one augmenting the other. During this technique both hips remain fully facing forward and again the body tensed, breath exhaled at the moment of contact.

1

2

3

4

21

AGE ZUKI
RISING PUNCH

Application

Age Zuki is a rising punch which makes use of the back of the fist and rises to contact the opponent UNDER the chin. It is performed in a similar way to the reverse punch, the main difference being, that the punching arm swings in a wide vertical arc.

As the technique nears its conclusion, the right (reverse) hip is thrust forward, the back leg is pushed back and the body tensed whilst exhaling via the mouth.

1

2

3

4

MAWASHI ZUKI
ROUNDHOUSE PUNCH

Mawashi Zuki may be performed as a stationary technique (Gyaku) or as a stepping punch depending on circumstances.

It follows an outward, circular rising path culminating in Seiken (Fore Fist) contacting the temple, at which time the hips should be rotated accordingly. The muscles should be tensed and exhalation takes place via the mouth.

Application

1

2

3

4

25

URA ZUKI
CLOSE PUNCH

Ura Zuki is a punch similar to Gyaku Zuki, except the punching arm remains bent on completion and the fist, inverted.
It travels in a straight line and the punch is complete when the punching arm elbow is about six inches from the hip. Ura Zuki is a lovely "Close In" fighting technique when directed at the Solar Plexus.

Application

1

2

3

4

27

TATE ZUKI
VERTICAL PUNCH

Tate Zuki is usually performed as a reverse (Gyaku) technique similar again to Gyaku Zuki. The same straight line is followed but this time, the fist turns only 90° – a quarter turn – and on completion, the punching arm remains slightly bent at the elbow. Exhalation and Kime are the same as preceding techniques.

Application

28

1

2

3

4

29

YAMA ZUKI
U PUNCH

Yama Zuki is a simultaneous multi level attack. From a left forward stance, put the right inverted fist by the waist and bring the left fist over the top of it, keeping it vertical. From this beginning position, direct the right fist upward and forward in a semi-circular fashion towards the opponent's face.
The right fist finishes with the back of the fist up, having revolved 180°.
The left fist pushes forward and inverted, attacks the solar plexus.
Both fists should reach the opponent together, therefore they should remain in a vertical line. A slight body inclination is necessary.

Application

1

2

3

4

31

KAGE ZUKI
HOOK PUNCH

Kage Zuki is ideal as a close in fighting body punch but with the fist finishing up in line with your body, it is necessary to step into your opponent to ensure its effectiveness. Used a great deal in Tekki Kata's, this technique is usually performed in Kiba Dachi. Special attention should be given to Kime, especially to the Deltoids and Latissimus Dorsi.

Application

1

2

3

4

STRIKING

Theoretical Considerations for Striking

Striking techniques involve the snapping action of the elbow and rely a great deal on the laws of action and reaction for their power. The force exerted in a striking action is increased by the snapping back effect of the arm, allowing the power of the strike to continue unimpeded to, or through its target. The strike will only be effective if the striking action coincides with the correct application of hips, exhalation and focus. Most strikes serve admirably as blocks too.

Class performing Knife Hand Strike from Heian Yondan, during outdoor training session.

SHUTŌ UCHI
KNIFE HAND STRIKE
(OUTSIDE)

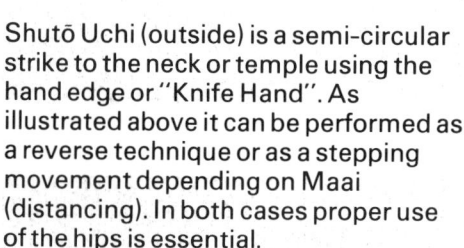

Shutō Uchi (outside) is a semi-circular strike to the neck or temple using the hand edge or "Knife Hand". As illustrated above it can be performed as a reverse technique or as a stepping movement depending on Maai (distancing). In both cases proper use of the hips is essential.

Application

1

2

3

4

37

SHUTŌ UCHI
KNIFE HAND STRIKE (INSIDE)

Shutō Uchi (inside) uses the same part of the hand as the outside technique but commences its movement with the striking hand cupping the opposite ear and the body is practically sideways on at the conclusion of the technique. Contact areas are the neck or temple.

Application

1

2

3

4

TETTSUI UCHI
BOTTOM FIST STRIKE

Tettsui Uchi can be used to attack most parts of the body. In the case of being grabbed by the wrist, one can use the swinging action of the arm to break the grip and continue over the head, so attacking the opponents skull with Tettsui Uchi.

Application

1

2

3

4

URAKEN UCHI
BACK FIST STRIKE

Application

Uraken Uchi has basically two forms. The first employs a lateral, semi-circular snapping action focusing the back fist on the opponent's temple. The second involves a semi-circular, overhead strike concentrating the power of the back fist onto the opponent's nose.

The former is a favourite technique for the "Pogo People" for in tournaments, the speed at which it can score can be devastating. A good example of the second occurs in Heian San Dan – or Seienchin.

1

2

3

4

43

HAITO UCHI
RIDGE HAND STRIKE (OUTSIDE)

Haito Uchi or ridge hand strike makes use of the opposite side of the hand to Shutō Uchi. The target area is the temple but make sure the thumb is not protruding out too far otherwise it may get broken. The striking hand swings round the body in a circular motion from a palm up to a palm down position. The beginner should understand straight line techniques before he attempts Haito Uchi, if not, he allows his elbow to go outside the body line when performing basic punches.

Application

1

2

3

4

HAITO UCHI
RIDGE HAND STRIKE (INSIDE)

Haito Uchi (inside) is often performed from the straddle leg stance, the striking hand moves from palm down to the palm up position and the target area can be the face, temple or neck. On completion of this technique, the body is side on.

Application

1

2

3

4

JŌDAN EMPI UCHI
UPPER ELBOW STRIKE

Jōdan Empi Uchi. The effective attacking range is drastically reduced when using elbow attacks as opposed to punches or strikes. Therefore Empi techniques have to be for close encounters. Jōdan Empi Uchi is very similar to Age Uke in many ways – certainly the action and reaction principle is the same. On completion, the elbow should have contacted under the chin and have the back of the fist turned out. Good hip movement is important.

Application

1

2

3

4

CHŪDAN EMPI UCHI
MIDDLE ELBOW STRIKE

Chūdan Empi Uchi may be performed on the spot as a Gyaku technique or indeed practised as a stepping movement. Either way, the hip movement is of great importance and on completion the attackers index finger knuckle of his striking arm should fit into the small of his chest (touching sternum).

Application

1

2

3

4

51

USHIRO CHŪDAN EMPI UCHI
REVERSE MIDDLE ELBOW STRIKE

Application

Ushiro Chūdan Empi Uchi. When attacking in the Gyaku position as in the illustration, the left hip must be back as far as possible so aiding the attacking elbow. The right hand assists for augmenting purposes. It is important to have the left fist facing palm up and the right hip pushed as far forward as possible. The beginner, when practising his first punch, Choku Zuki, inadvertently performs a reverse elbow strike.

1

2

3

4

53

YOKO CHŪDAN EMPI UCHI
SIDE MIDDLE ELBOW STRIKE

Yoko Chūdan Empi Uchi is generally performed in the Kiba Dachi stance and the opponent's sternum makes a fine target for this penetrating technique. On completion, the back of the fist remains up and care should be taken to control very carefully when practising, as sternums have a nasty habit of breaking.

Application

1

2

3

4

BLOCKING

Theoretical Considerations for Blocking

Blocking consists of parrying or deflecting blows in such a way as to leave the defender unharmed, and in an advantageous position to counter attack successfully. The attacking limb will have its course altered by the influence of the blocking arm or leg moving in an upwards, downwards or sideways direction.

Advanced training class in progress (Chūdan Uchi Ude Uke)

AGE UKE
UPPER RISING BLOCK

Application

Age Uke is one of the most basic Shotokan blocks. Points to remember are these:
The blocking arm should rise from the waist at an angle of 45°. The arm and fist turn 180° at the end of the technique as contact is made. When pulling the opposite arm down, make sure the elbow pulls down in the direction of the hip. On completion, the hips and body must be 45° to the front and the back leg must be pushed straight on contact.

1

2

3

4

SOTO UDE UKE
OUTSIDE FOREARM BLOCK

Application

Soto Ude Uke is perhaps the strongest mid section block of all. On occasions it can be used to block kicks with surprising effectiveness.
The block starts its life at Jōdan level pulled well back past the head. It travels from that position, in a semi circle to a spot roughly in front of the chest and on completion, the wrist turns 180° just prior to Kime. Both body and hips turn 45° into Hanmi.

1

2

3

4

UCHI UDE UKE
INSIDE FOREARM BLOCK

Application

Uchi Ude Uke is a lot easier to perform than Soto Ude Uke as far as beginners are concerned. The blocking arm starts from above the opposite hip – back of the fist up – and swings in an arc across the body. It finishes its journey in line with the side of the body, the elbow being bent at a 90° angle and the top of the fist in line with the shoulder. The body and hips twist to the 45° position as the block is completed.

1

2

3

4

MOROTE UKE
AUGMENTED FOREARM BLOCK

Application

Morote Uke is an inside forward block augmented and strengthened by having the opposite arm to assist it. Indeed, the augmenting arm is quite interesting in so far as it hangs loosely by the side of the body, almost being left behind, then finally accelerates to catch the blocking arm up.

In touching the blocking arm just inside the elbow it strengthens the block quite considerably for it brings into play the muscles on that side of the body and promotes increased harmony.

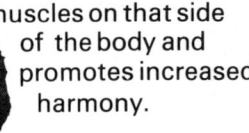

1

2

3

4

SHUTO UKE
KNIFE HAND BLOCK

Application

Shutō Uke – This technique is more difficult than most, therefore it often gets neglected by beginner and high grade alike. Points to remember are: Keep the blocking arm at a 45° angle, otherwise, one may miss the punch completely. The opposite hand should strike the solar plexus as it pulls back. This will assist in Kime. Keep the body and hips at 45° and try not to let the back knee turn in.

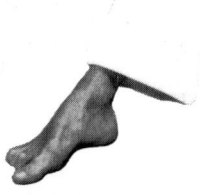

1

2

3

4

TATE SHUTŌ
VERTICAL KNIFE HAND BLOCK

Application

Tate Shutō is a block utilising the knife hand edge. One needs to be a little more confident when using this technique as opposed to the more conventional blocks. However, once the student has become reasonably accurate, this block will begin to appeal more. It can be used to attack inside or outside an opponent's arm and prepares the way for a rapid counter punch.

1

2

3

4

JŪJI UKE
X BLOCK (JŌDAN)

Jūji Uke is a very strong double handed blocking technique that can be performed Jōdan or Gedan.
In this, the Jōdan version, the hands rise from the hips at 45° and lock together, crossed above the head. The technique, illustrated here, is called Haishu Jūji Uke, for the back of the hands make contact with the attacker's arm. If performed from a left forward stance, it is important to have the right hip forward as the block concludes.

Application

1

2

3

4

JŪJI UKE
X BLOCK (GEDAN)

Jūji Uke (Gedan) is a double block used in conjunction with the hips, to stop a front kick and simultaneously attack the shin bone. It really consists of two techniques – Gedan Barai and Tate Zuki. To ensure success, this block needs to be executed quickly, stopping the kicking leg in its tracks and preventing it from gaining speed and momentum.

Application

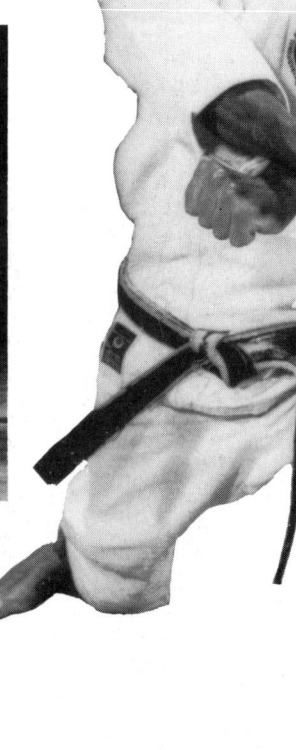

1

2

3

4

73

GEDAN BARAI
DOWNWARD BLOCK

Application

Gedan Barai – The most basic of blocks is probably used and practised more than any other technique. Usually performed in Zenkutsu Dachi, it makes maximum use of the arms, legs, body and hips. Most lessons involve many Gedan Barai's – it's the first technique from the very first Kata and it's still there in the most advanced one. Yes – the left Gedan Barai is most people's strongest block – what about the right one?

1

2

3

4

KAKIWAKE UKE
WEDGE BLOCK

Application

Kakiwake Uke, the last of our basic blocks is a wedge block, which, after training, is a very effective defence against being grabbed by the coat lapels. Its effective execution depends mainly on being able to contract the Hara and the muscles at the side of the body.

On completion, it leaves the attacker's body wide open and his position is extremely vulnerable, having both hands and arms outside yours.

1

2

3

4

KICKING

Theoretical Considerations for Kicking

Kicking uses the whole of one's body to the maximum and the hips especially play a major role in executing the various techniques. Basically, there are three types of kicks: Snap kicks, thrust kicks and striking kicks. In this book, we have tried to show a representative example from each group but have covered only the basic kicks needed by the beginner.

Snap kicks depend for their success on snapping the leg straight from the knee and then back again as quickly as possible. Once raised, the knee is used as a fulcrum for a semi-circular movement. Thrust kicks rely on raising the knee first and then thrusting the leg straight using the force of the hip for additional power.

Striking kicks may be used for blocking or attacking and their main virtue is flexibility. Balance is a key factor in kicking and keeping the sole of the supporting foot firmly on the floor ensures maximum stability.

A good tip is to aim the knee at the target – the foot should automatically follow.

Class performing Mawashi Geri during outdoor training session

MAE GERI
FRONT KICK

Mae Geri, a front kick performed from Zenkutsu Dachi is a snapkick acquiring its power from the snapping action of the lower leg aided by the application of the hips. Basically there are three positions that constitute this kick. Firstly, the kicking leg knee is raised in front and to the centre of the body. Secondly, the leg is straightened, hips applied, instep straightened and toes curled back.

Thirdly, the leg is snapped back assuming the first position and with the hips returned to *their* original position, the back should be straight and balance maintained.

Application

1

2

3

4

YOKO GERI KEAGE
SIDE SNAP KICK

Yoko Geri Keage is another snap kick but this time the kicking leg travels to the side of the body. Usually performed from a Kiba Dachi, the kicking leg knee is first raised to the side, then the leg is straightened and at this point, the hip rises up to augment the snapping action. Finally, the leg is snapped back – hip lowered and the stance resumed. The striking point is the foot edge (Sokuto).

Application

1

2

3

4

YOKO GERI KEKOMI
SIDE THRUST KICK

Yoko Geri Kekomi utilises the thrusting action of the leg augmented by the hip. It is more of a "Total Commitment" technique and requires good control and balance keeping the recovery factor in mind. As with Keage, the striking point is Sokuto. An important point to bear in mind is the pivoting action on the ball of the supporting foot as the thrusting takes place. Failure to do this could result in a damaged cartilage in the knee of that supporting leg.

Application

1

2

3

4

MAWASHI GERI
ROUNDHOUSE KICK

Mawashi Geri is a semi circular snap kick using the ball of the foot (Koshi) as the striking point. From a Zenkutsu Dachi, raise the knee sideways keeping the leg bent and the toes curled up. Then snap the leg forward aiming the foot at the target, at the same time allowing the hips to rotate. Immediately the leg has straightened, snap it back together with the hips to their original position. At all times endeavour to keep the knee higher than the foot.

Application

1

2

3

4

87

USHIRO GERI
REVERSE KICK

Ushiro Geri makes use of the thrusting action of the leg, aided by the hips in a rearward direction. Usually performed as a spinning technique using the heel as a striking point, Ushiro Geri takes the face of the person kicking furthest away from the attacker and encourages him to commit himself to the technique much more. However, this commitment in competitions may result in disqualification through excessive contact. Both hips should be thrust back simultaneously, as in Oi Zuki or Mae Geri.

Application

1

2

3

4

89

MIKAZUKI GERI UKE
CRESCENT KICK BLOCK

Mikazuki-Geri Uke may be used as a block or an attack using the sole of the foot as a striking point. Endeavour to keep the knee parallel to the floor when performing this circular movement.

Application

1

2

3

4

MIKAZUKI GERI
CRESCENT KICK

Mikazuki Geri performed as a block or an attack utilises the ball of the foot (Koshi) and the kick takes its name from the crescent like action of the leg whether moving in an inward or outward direction. The thigh of the kicking leg should remain parallel to the floor if possible.

Application

1

2

3

4

93

USHIRO MAWASHI GERI
REVERSE ROUNDHOUSE KICK

Ushiro-Mawashi-Geri. This is a reverse roundhouse kick using the heel as the striking point. Some styles prefer to contact with the sole of the foot. This certainly is the case in tournaments for obvious reasons. Bring the kicking leg up and round, rotating the hips and body to enable the heel to make contact with the back of the neck or back area in the case of Chūdan.

Application

1

2

3

4

KARATE IS FOR EV

Simon Carter (right) and Jonathan Trower two of Task's Junior Black Belts.

Today's children – tomorrows instructors, having a great time and actually laughing at one of Sensei's jokes.

TO BE ENJOYED BY Y

RYONE – FOR LIFE!

A recent ladies self defence course at "Unilever", Bedford.

Some of Task's ladies watch Mrs. Sue Sylvester 2nd Dan from Flitwick, demonstrate an arm lever to an unsuspecting male.

UNG AND OLD ALIKE!

PART 2 KATA
FORMAL EXERCISE

Kata have been with us for a long time, probably since the Sixth Century. What is remarkable, is that they have endured to this day. True – the techniques may have changed somewhat over the years due to external pressures and influences from the great masters of the past, but the fact remains, they are practised for the same reasons today as they were them. In a nutshell – "The Perfection of Character".
Kata offers so much – to so many by way of physical and mental training.
All the Katas in this book have at least one thing in common – they all begin with defensive movements – to show humility, on the practitioner's part. Their influence overall through physical exercise and breath control directly affect longevity of life. This is borne out by the advanced age to which many masters live.
By continually striving to improve and perfect the techniques in Kata, a person's attitude, mind and character are indirectly improved. Another point often overlooked by many Karateka and one, more profound by far than any other, is this – "a student training in a Dojo, no matter what country, in 1983 could be training in the same techniques as his predecessor was 1,000 years before him. In these days of change and modernisation, how nice it is to be involved in an art *that has truly stood "The Test of Time"*.

The following ten elements of Kata as taught by Kanazawa Sensei, must be well practised and understood in order to obtain maximum benefit:

- **Yoi No Kisin** – the spirit of getting ready. The concentration of will and mind against the opponent as a preliminary to the movements of the Kata.
- **Inyo** – the active and passive. Always keeping in mind both attack and defence.
- **Chikara No Kyojaku** – the manner of using strength. The degree of power used for each movement and position in Kata.
- **Waza No Kankyu** – the speed of movement. The speed used for each movement and position in Kata.
- **Tai No Shinshuku** – the degree of expansion or contraction. The degree of expansion or contraction of the body in each movement and position in Kata.
- **Kokyu** – breathing. Breath control related to the posture and movement in Kata.
- **Tyakugan** – the aiming points. In Kata you must keep the purpose of the movement in mind.
- **Kiai** – shouting. Shouting at set points in Kata to demonstrate the martial spirit.
- **Keitai No Hoji** – correct positioning. Correct positioning in movement and stance.
- **Zanshin** – remaining on guard. Remaining on guard at the completion of the Kata (i.e. back to "Yoi") until told to relax "Enoy".

TAIKYOKU SHODAN

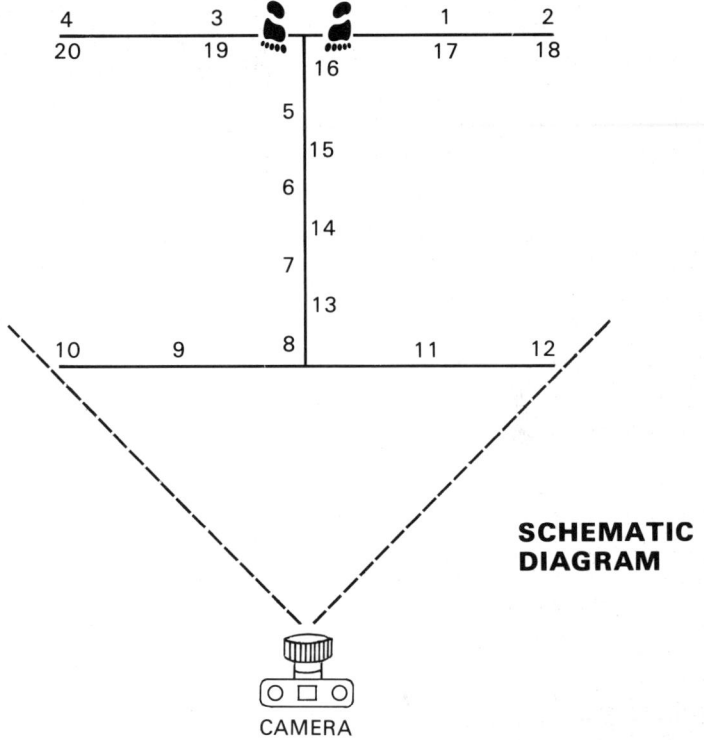

SCHEMATIC DIAGRAM

CAMERA

Of the three Taikyoku forms, Shōdan is the most elementary and consists of one block, one attack and one stance.

Once someone is able to perform the Taikyoku forms with proficiency, he can understand the other Kata with relative ease.

To quote Funakoshi: "Because of its simplicity the Kata is easily learned by beginners, nevertheless, as its name implies*, this form is of the most profound character and one to which, upon mastery of the art of Karate, an expert will return to select it as the ultimate training Kata".

* Taikyoku is a philosophical term denoting the macrocosm before its differentiation into heaven and earth: hence, chaos or the void.

Left: Hidari Gedan Barai

YOI

1

HIDARI GEDAN BARAI

FAST

FAST

3

MIGI GEDAN BARAI

4

HIDARI OI ZUKI

FAST

2

MIGI OI ZUKI

FAST

5

HIDARI GEDAN BARAI

FAST

FAST

6
MIGI OI ZUKI

7
HIDARI OI ZUKI

FAST

FAST

9
HIDARI GEDAN BARAI

10
MIGI OI ZUKI

FAST  **KIAI**

8

MIGI OI ZUKI

FAST

11

MIGI GEDAN BARAI

FAST

FAST

12
HIDARI OI ZUKI

13
HIDARI GEDAN BARAI

FAST

FAST **KIAI**

15
HIDARI OI ZUKI

16
MIGI OI ZUKI

FAST

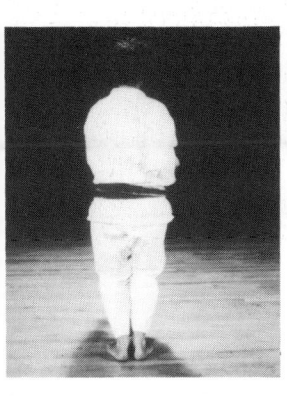  

14

MIGI OI ZUKI

FAST

17

HIDARI GEDAN BARAI

FAST

FAST

18

MIGI OI ZUKI

19

MIGI GEDAN BARAI

YAME

108

FAST

20

HIDARI OI ZUKI

Masaaki Ueki - **Y. Takahashi** - **Keigo Abe** (left to right) Three of the author's favourite instructors pictured here at the old J.K.A. headquarters in Tokyo in 1967. **Takahashi Sensei** (centre), liked by everyone and renowned for his superb technique, **died tragically in a road accident** soon after this picture was taken.

109

13-16 FRONT VIEW

FAST

FAST

13

HIDARI GEDAN BARAI

14

MIGI OI ZUKI

FAST ⚡ **KIAI**

16

MIGI OI ZUKI

FAST

15

HIDARI OI ZUKI

The author pictured here with Chris Burton 4th Dan at a recent course in **Okinawan "Sai"** put on by Sensei for over 60 Task Black Belts.

APPLICATIONS

A1 **A2**

B1 **B2**

C1 **C2**

112

TAIKYOKU SHODAN

A3

A4

B3

B4

B5

C3

C4

TAIKYOKU SHODAN

YOI

1

2

6

7

8 KIAI

12

13

14

18

19

20

KIAI

YAME

115

HEIAN SHODAN

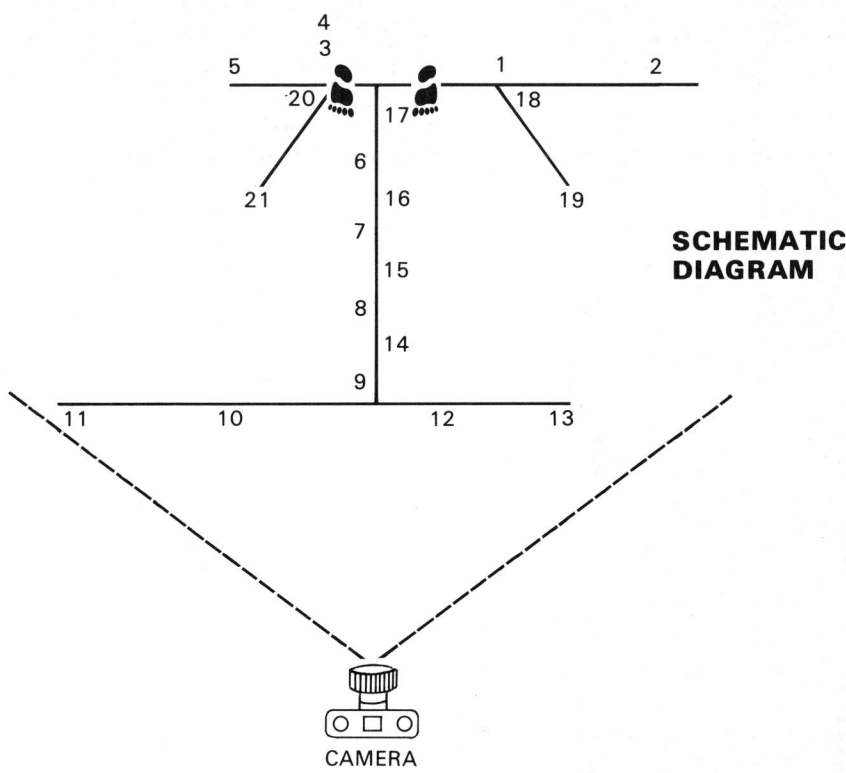

SCHEMATIC DIAGRAM

CAMERA

The word Heian means "Peaceful Mind", Heian Sho Dan being the first of five Heian Katas. It has 21 movements and takes about 40 seconds to perform.

Students should concentrate on perfecting the forward and back stances in this Kata. For the first time, Shutō Uke is introduced together with Age Uke and Tettsui Uchi. Sensei Itosu, the man credited with the compilation of the Heian Katas in the early 1900s set great store in the proficient execution of this Kata.

Left: Migi Jodan Age Uke

YOI

1

HIDARI GEDAN BARAI

3

MIGI GEDAN BARAI

4

MIGI TETTSUI UCHI

2

MIGI OI ZUKI

5

HIDARI OI ZUKI

6

HIDARI GEDAN BARAI

7

MIGI AGE UKE

9

MIGI AGE UKE

10

HIDARI GEDAN BARAI

FAST

8

HIDARI AGE UKE

FAST

11

MIGI OI ZUKI

FAST

FAST

12
MIGI GEDAN BARAI

13
HIDARI OI ZUKI

FAST

FAST

15
MIGI OI ZUKI

16
HIDARI OI ZUKI

FAST

  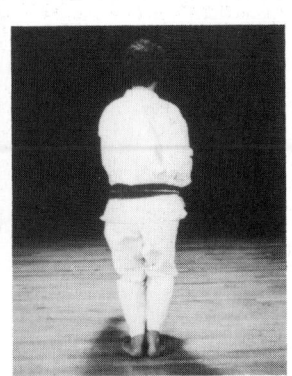

14

HIDARI GEDAN BARAI

FAST  **KIAI**

17

MIGI OI ZUKI

123

18
HIDARI SHUTŌ UKE

19
MIGI SHUTŌ UKE

21
HIDARI SHUTŌ UKE

YAME

FAST

20

MIGI SHUTŌ UKE

The British contingent photographed here with the Japanese Wado Ryu instructors at the first Japan Karate Masters Seminar in 1985. Present are: Oliver Brunton (Wado Ryu), John Smith (Bujinkai), Brian Smith (Shukokai), Bernard Creton (Kyokushin), Barry Wilkinson (Wado Ryu), Terry Pottage (Kenukai), John van Weenen (Shotokan), Lee Costa (Kyokushin), Dickie Dowler, Steve and Tommy Morris

125

MOVEMENTS 14-17

FAST

FAST

14

HIDARI GEDAN BARAI

15

MIGI OI ZUKI

FAST

KIAI

17

MIGI OI ZUKI

FRONT VIEW

FAST

16

HIDARI OI ZUKI

The author at a Zen monastery near Yokohama in 1968

127

APPLICATIONS

A1

A2

A6

B1

C1

C2

C3

D1

D2

D3

HEIAN SHODAN

A3
A4
A5

B2
B3
B4

TAI SABAKI

C4

HEIAN SHODAN

YOI   1   2

6   7   8

12   13   14

18   19   20

3   4   5

KIAI 9   10   11

15   16   **KIAI** 17

21   **YAME**

HEIAN NIDAN

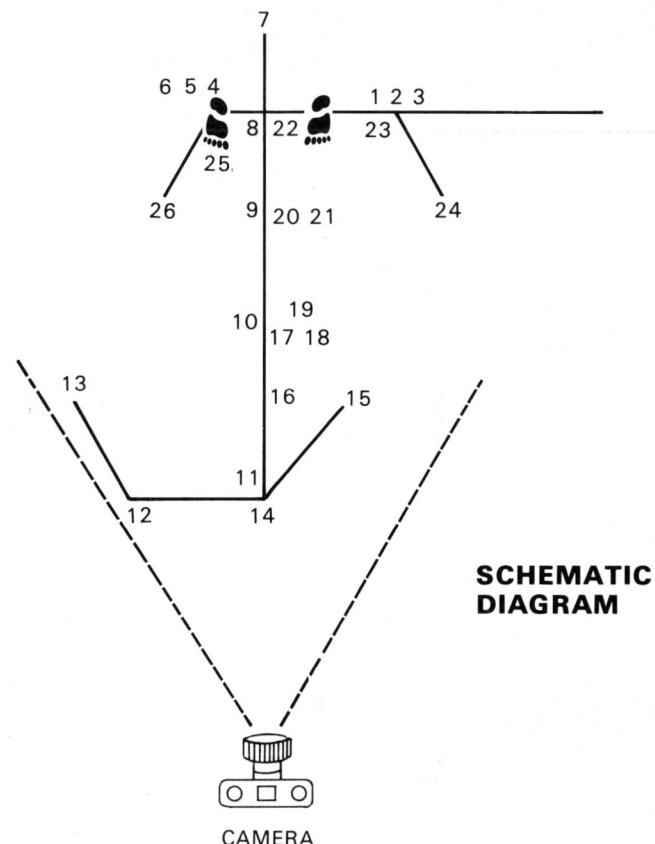

SCHEMATIC DIAGRAM

CAMERA

Heian Nidan carries on where Heian Shodan left off. Having learned the back stance, it is now used to open the Kata and performs in conjunction with Haiwan-Jōdan-Uke. We also see the arrival of techniques like Ura Zuki, Uraken Uchi, Shihon Nukite, and kicking techniques begin to appear in the form of Mae Geri and Yoko Geri. An interesting point concerns the change of direction when executing Yoko Geri Keage.

This Kata requires about 40 seconds to complete the 26 movements.

Left: Migi Chūdan Shihon Nukite

YOI

1

**HIDARI JŌDAN
HAIWAN UKE**

FAST

3

HIDARI CHŪDAN ZUKI

134

FAST

4

**MIGI JŌDAN
HAIWAN UKE**

FAST

2

MIGI URA ZUKI

FAST

5

HIDARI URA ZUKI

FAST

FAST

6

MIGI CHŪDAN ZUKI

7

YOKO KEAGE-URAKEN

FAST

FAST

9

MIGI SHUTŌ UKE

10

HIDARI SHUTŌ UKE

FAST

8

HIDARI SHUTŌ UKE

FAST **KIAI**

11

**MIGI CHUDAN SHIHON
NUKITE – KIAI**

FAST

FAST

12

HIDARI SHUTŌ UKE

13

MIGI SHUTŌ UKE

FAST

FAST

15

HIDARI SHUTŌ UKE

16

**MIGI
UCHI UKE**

**GYAKU
HANMI**

138

FAST

14

MIGI SHUTŌ UKE

FAST

17

**MIGI
MAE GERI**

18

**HIDARI CHŪDAN
GYAKU ZUKI**

19

**HIDARI CHŪDAN
UCHI UKE
GYAKU HANMI**

21

**MIGI CHŪDAN
GYAKU ZUKI**

22

**MIGI CHŪDAN
MOROTE UKE**

20

HIDARI MAE GERI

23

**HIDARI
GEDAN BARAI**

FAST **FAST**

24

MIGI AGE UKE

25

MIGI GEDAN BARAI

YAME

142

FAST

26
HIDARI AGE UKE KIAI

15·16 FRONT VIEW

A   **B**   **C**   **D**

17-22 FRONT VIEW

FAST

FAST

17

MIGI MAE GERI

18

HIDARI GYAKU ZUKI

FAST

FAST

20

HIDARI MAE GERI

21

MIGI GYAKU ZUKI

FAST

19

HIDARI UCHI UKE

FAST

22

MIGI MOROTE UKE

APPLICATIONS

HEIAN NIDAN

HEIAN NIDAN

YOI   1   2

6   7   8

12   13   14

18   19   20

24   25   26

KIAI

148

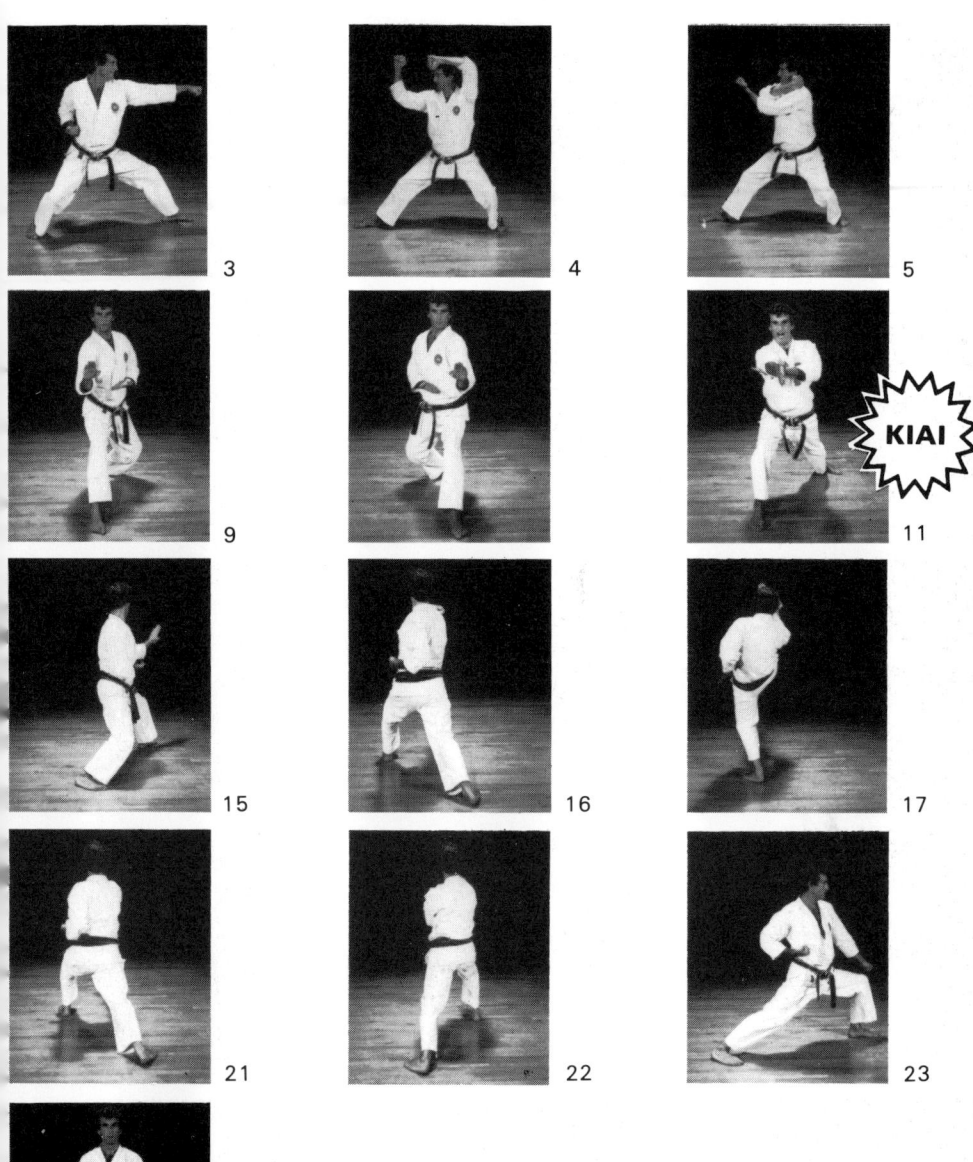

3

4

5

9

11

KIAI

15

16

17

21

22

23

YAME

149

HEIAN SANDAN

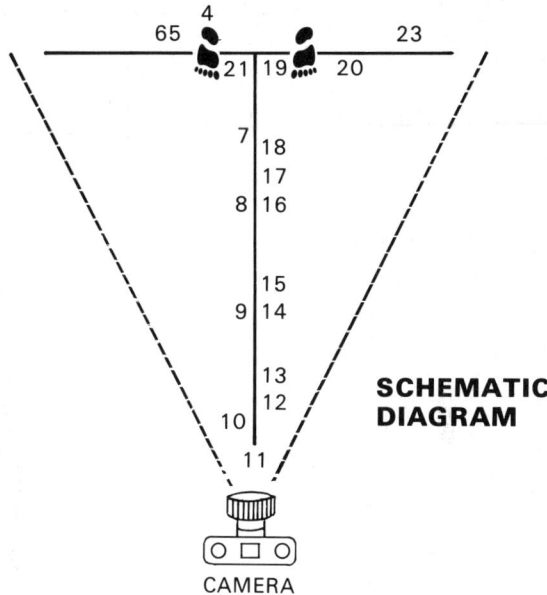

SCHEMATIC DIAGRAM

CAMERA

Heian Sandan begins with Chudan Uchi Uke again performed in Kokutsu Dachi and is followed by Kosa Uke, which in my opinion has been introduced perhaps a little prematurely. Using Kōsa Uke to Block either a Mae Geri or an Oi Zuki is fair enough, despite the degree of difficulty in synchronisation and harmony, however, blocking Yama Zuki is a different kettle of fish and requires much practise together with an ability to "Kime" and relax speedily, ready for the next attack and corresponding Kōsa Uke.

For the first time in Kata, we see the appearance of Fumikomi and Empi Uke and the simultaneous attack of Ushiro Empi and Tate Zuki.

The 21 movements should take 40 seconds to complete.

Left: Hidari Tate Zuki – Migi Empi

YOI

1

HIDARI CHŪDAN UCHI UKE

3

KŌSA UKE

4

MIGI CHŪDAN UCHI UKE

152

FAST

2

KŌSA UKE

FAST

5

KŌSA UKE

FAST

FAST

6

KŌSA UKE

7

HIDARI MOROTE UKE

FAST

FAST ✦ **KIAI**

9

HIDARI TETTSUI UCHI

10

MIGI CHŪDAN OI ZUKI

8

MIGI SHIHON NUKITE

SLOW

11

**RYOKEN
KOSHI GAMAE**

12

MIGI EMPI UKE

13

JŌDAN URAKEN UCHI

15

HIDARI URAKEN UCHI

16

MIGI EMPI UKE

FAST

14

HIDARI EMPI UKE

FAST

17

MIGI URAKEN UCHI

SLOW **FAST**

18

MIGI CHŪDAN TATE SHUTO UKE

19

HIDARI CHŪDAN OI ZUKI

FAST KIAI

21

HIDARI TATE ZUKI MIGI EMPI

YAME

FAST

20
**MIGI TATE ZUKI
HIDARI EMPI**

19-20 FRONT VIEW

19
**HIDARI CHŪDAN
OI ZUKI**

20
**MIGI TATE ZUKI
HIDARI EMPI**

11-19 FRONT VIEW

SLOW

FAST

11
RYOKEN KOSHI
GAMAE

12
MIGI EMPI UKE

FAST

FAST

14
HIDARI EMPI UKE

15
HIDARI URAKEN UCHI

FAST

SLOW

17
MIGI URAKEN UCHI

18
MIGI CHŪDAN TATE
SHUTO UKE

FAST

13

JŌDAN URAKEN UCHI

FAST

16

MIGI EMPI UCHI

FAST

19

HIDARI CHŪDAN OI ZUKI

APPLICATIONS

A1

A2

A3

B1

B2

B3

B7

D1

C1

C2

C3

HEIAN SANDAN

A4

A5

A6

B4

B5

B6

D2

D3

C4

HEIAN SANDAN

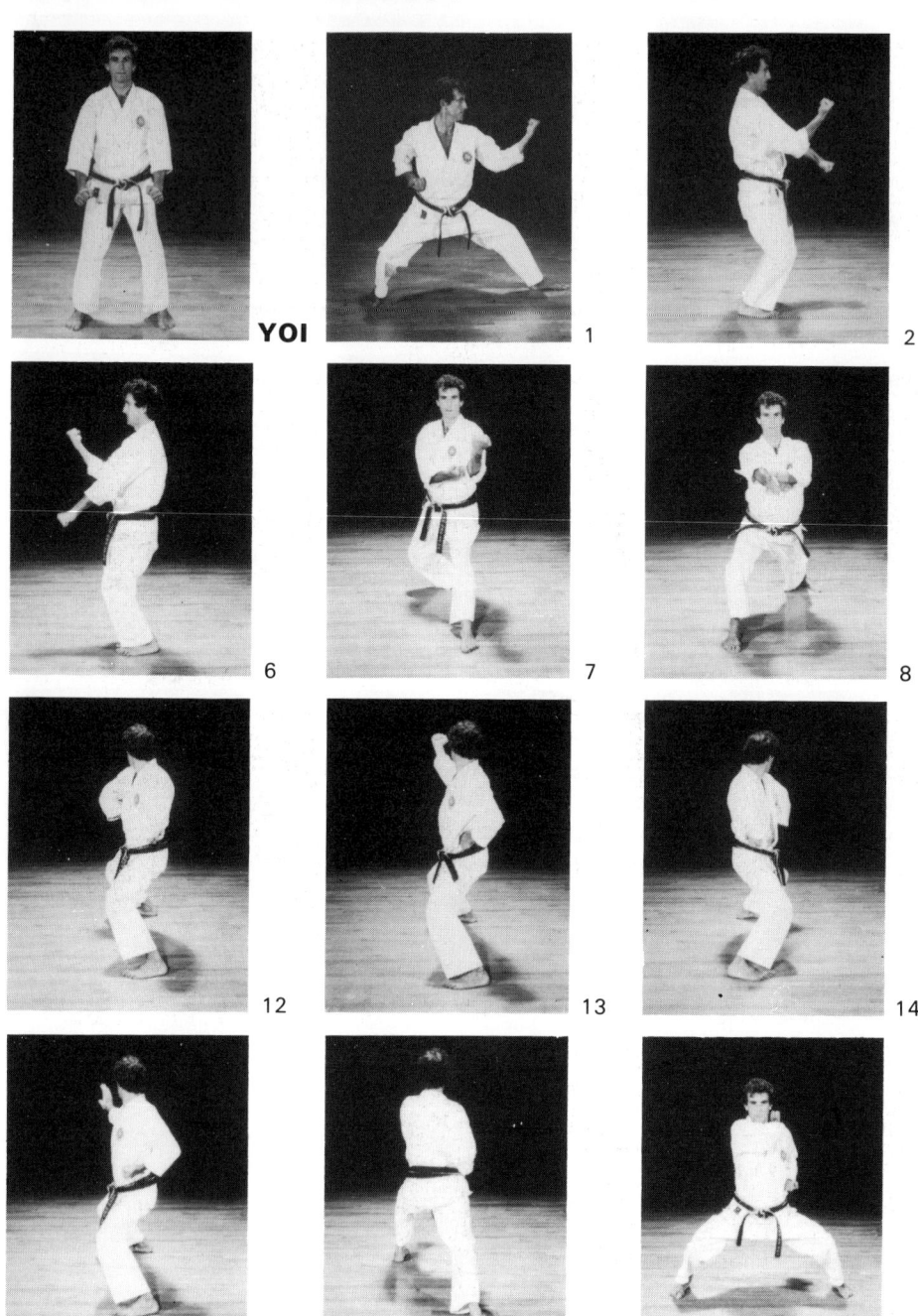

YOI   1   2

6   7   8

12   13   14

18   19   20

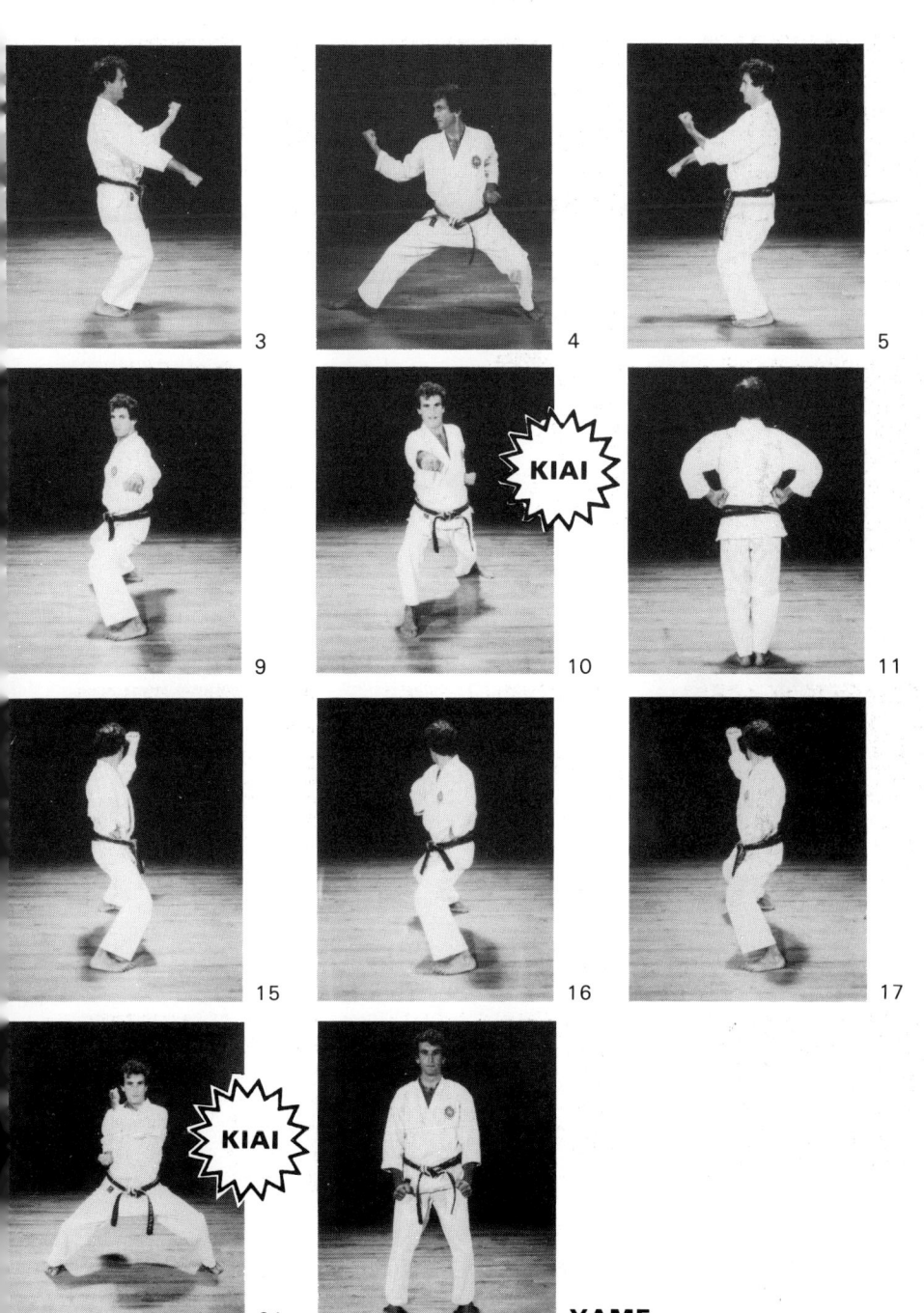

3

4

5

9

KIAI

10

11

15

16

17

KIAI

21

YAME

HEIAN YONDAN

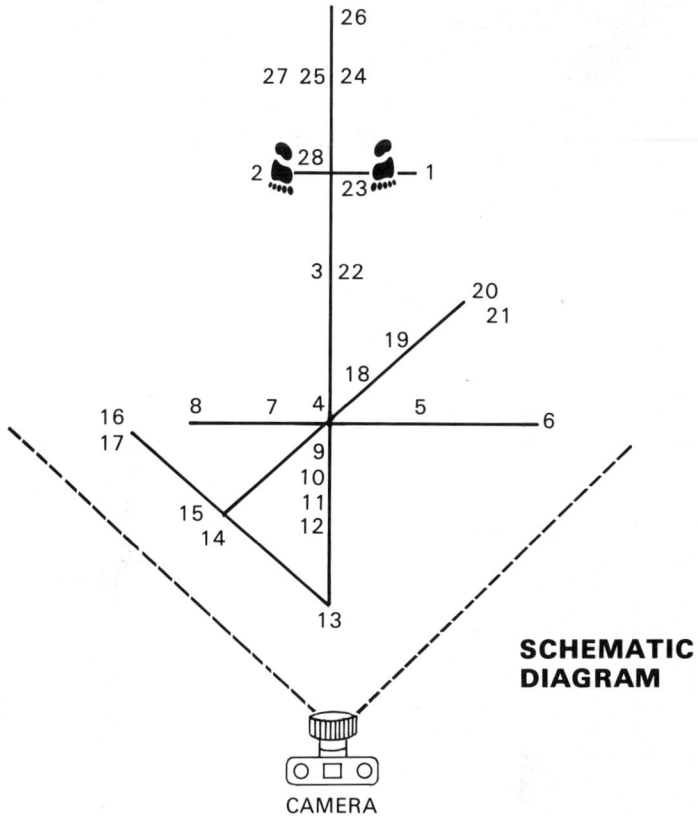

SCHEMATIC DIAGRAM

CAMERA

Heian Yondan provides the most variation of any Heian Kata and with it, the awareness of the vast number of techniques to be mastered in the future.

Beginning with Haishu Haiwan Uke one learns to harmonise the arms together, develop the power in the block by augmenting one arm with the other, giving the student the opportunity to develop "kime" " through dynamic tension. Appearing for the first time are Juji Uke, Gedan Shutō, Shutō Uchi, Kakiwake Uke and Hiza Geri.

When performing Hiza Geri, equal concentration and power distribution must take place when attacking with the right knee and pulling the head down onto it with both hands. It is important to contract the Hara and use to the optimum the muscles at the side of the body. (Latissimus Dorsi).

Left: Migi Jodan Mae Geri

YOI

1

HAISHU HAIWAN UKE

FAST

FAST

3

GEDAN JUJI UKE

4

**MIGI CHŪDAN
MOROTE UKE**

SLOW 4–5 SECONDS
LONG INHALATION

2

HAISHU HAIWAN UKE

FAST

5

YOKO KEAGE
URAKEN
UCHI

169

6

MIGI MAE EMPI

7

**YOKO KEAGE
URAKEN UCHI**

9

**HIDARI GEDAN
SHUTŌ BARAI**

10

**MIGI JŌDAN
SHUTŌ UCHI**

FAST

8

HIDARI MAE EMPI

FAST

11

**MIGI JŌDAN
MAE GERI**

171

11–12–13 ARE ALL ONE MOVEMENT BUT SHOWN HERE SEPARATELY TO AVOID CONFUSION

FAST

FAST KIAI

12

HIDARI TEISHO UKE

13

**MIGI CHŪDAN
URAKEN UCHI**

FAST

FAST

16

**MIGI JŌDAN
MAE GERI**

MIGI CHŪDAN OI ZUKI

14

CHŪDAN KAKIWAKE UKE

FAST

17

**HIDARI CHŪDAN
GYAKU ZUKI**

**SLOW 4–5 SECONDS
LONG EXHALATION**

FAST

18

**CHŪDAN KAKIWAKE
UKE**

19

**HIDARI JŌDAN MAE
GERI**

FAST

FAST

21

**MIGI CHŪDAN
GYAKU ZUKI**

22

**HIDARI CHUDAN
MOROTE UKE**

FAST

20

**HIDARI CHŪDAN
OI ZUKI**

FAST

23

**MIGI CHŪDAN
MOROTE UKE**

24

HIDARI CHŪDAN MOROTE UKE

25

MOROTE KUBI OSAE

27

HIDARI CHŪDAN SHUTŌ UKE

28

MIGI CHŪDAN SHUTŌ UKE

176

26

MIGI HIZA GERI UCHI

YAME

177

21-26 FRONT VIEW

FAST

FAST

21

**MIGI CHŪDAN
GYAKU ZUKI**

22

**HIDARI CHŪDAN
MOROTE UKE**

FAST

FAST

24

**HIDARI CHŪDAN
MOROTE UKE**

25

MOROTE KUBI OSAE

FAST

23

**MIGI CHŪDAN
MOROTE UKE**

FAST **KIAI**

26

**MIGI HIZA
GERI UCHI**

APPLICATIONS

BLOCKING   **GRABBING**   **STRIKING**

A1   A2   A3

BLOCKING   **STRIKING**

B4   B5

KICKING

C1

PUNCHING   **PUNCHING**

D3   D4

BLOCKING

E1

HEIAN YONDAN

BLOCKING   BLOCKING & STRIKING   KICKING

B1   B2   B3

STRIKING   GRABBING   KICKING

C2   D1   D2

GRABBING   KICKING

E2   E3

HEIAN YONDAN

YOI

1

2

6

7

8

12

KIAI

13

14

18

19

20

24

25

KIAI

26

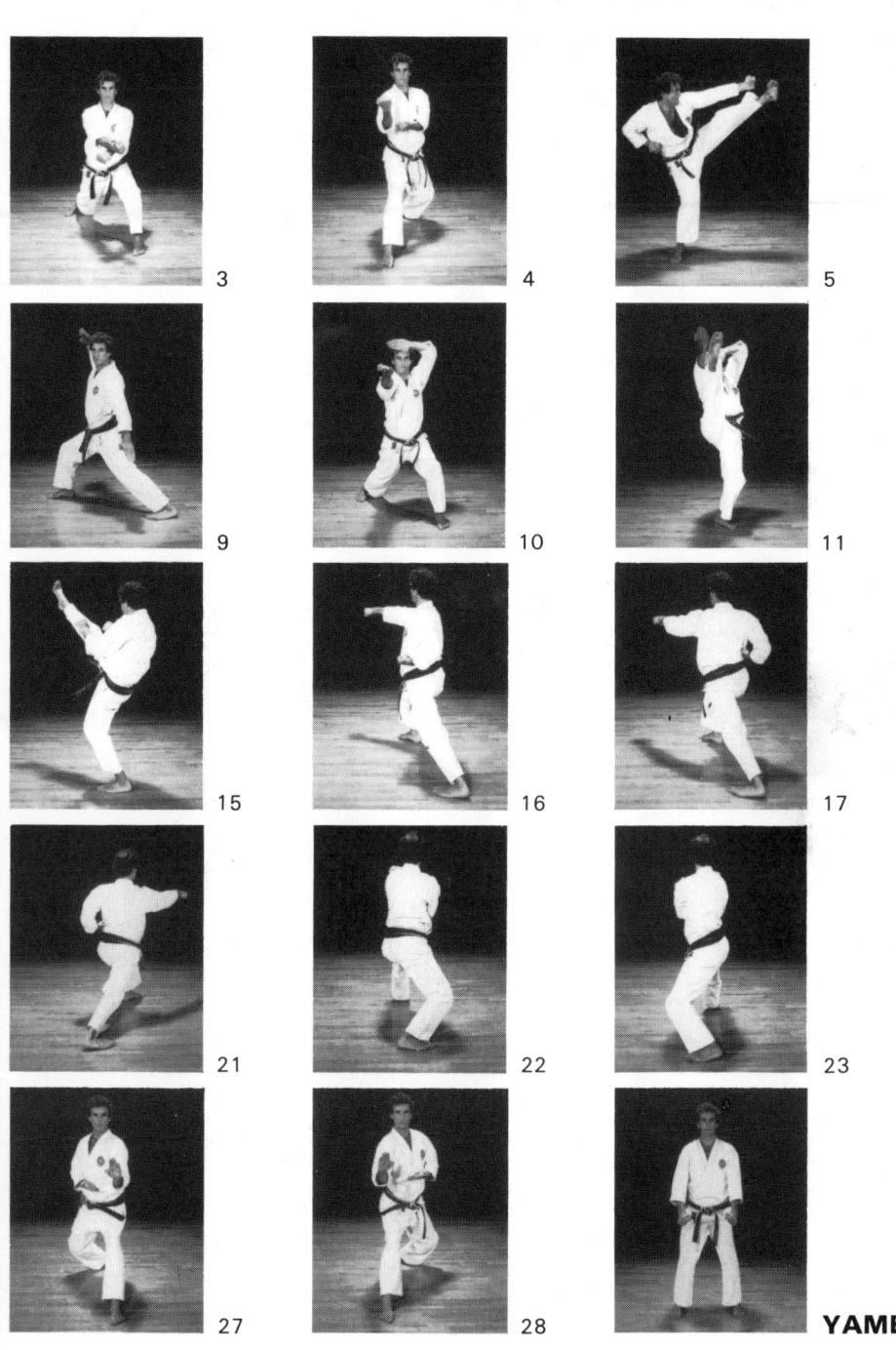

3

4

5

9

10

11

15

16

17

21

22

23

27

28

YAME

HEIAN GŌDAN

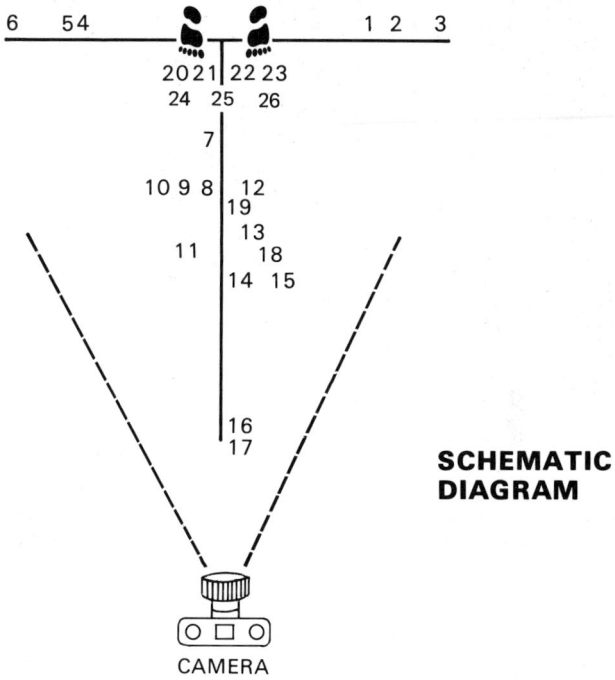

SCHEMATIC
DIAGRAM

CAMERA

Heian Go Dan introduces the student to many new techniques, none more important than Mizuno-Nagare-No-Kamae – The Flowing Water Technique. This technique is of course for punching but has spiritual connotations. The Forearm, although parallel to the chest, should be inclined slightly downwards with the feeling of water flowing down the arm from the shoulder.

For the first time we see Jōdan Haishu Juji Uke, Morote Tsuki Age and Gedan Nukite.

Jumping over a "Bo" attack to avoid having the legs broken provides an adequate and new experience in Karate movements.

There are 26 movements and they should occupy about 50 seconds.

Left: Migi Mikazuki Geri

YOI

1

**HIDARI CHŪDAN
UCHI UKE**

**LONG INHALATION
SLOW**

FAST

3

HIDARI KAGI GAMAE

4

MIGI CHŪDAN UCHI UKE

2

**MIGI CHŪDAN
GYAKU ZUKI**

5

**HIDARI CHŪDAN
GYAKU ZUKI**

6

MIGI KAGI GAMAE

7

**MIGI CHŪDAN
MOROTE UKE**

FAST

FAST

9

**JODAN HAISHU
JUJI UKE**

10

CHŪDAN OSAE UKE

188

FAST

8
GEDAN JUJI UKE

FAST **KIAI**

11
**CHŪDAN MIGI
OI ZUKI**

12
MIGI GEDAN BARAI

13
CHŪDAN HAISHU UKE

FAST

FAST

15
MIGI MAE EMPI

16
**MIGI CHŪDAN
MOROTE UKE**

FAST

14

MIGI MIKAZUKI GERI

FAST

17

**KŌHŌ TSUKI
AGE**

18

JUMPING OVER BO

19

GEDAN JŪJI UKE

21

**MIGI GEDAN
SHUTŌ UCHI**

22

**MANJI GAMAE
IN KŌKUTSU DACHI**

FAST

20
**MIGI CHŪDAN
MOROTE UKE**

**LONG INHALATION
SLOW**

23
**MANJI GAMAE
IN HEISOKU DACHI**

24

**MANJI GAMAE
IN HEISOKU DACHI**

25

**HIDARI GEDAN
SHUTŌ UCHI**

27

YAME

FAST

26

MANJI GAMAE
IN KŌKUTSU DACHI

The author with **Hakaoshi Sensei 7th Dan Wado Ryu** on a course at Shiga 300 miles south of Tokyo in 1985.

19-20 FRONT VIEW

FAST   **FAST**

GEDAN JUJI UKE   **MIGI CHŪDAN
                                                  MOROTE UKE**

11-12 SIDE VIEW

FAST   **FAST**

CHŪDAN MIGI OI ZUKI   **MIGI GEDAN BARAI**

APPLICATIONS

YOI	BLOCKING	PUNCHING
A1	A2	A3

BLOCKING A KICK	BLOCKING A PUNCH	BLOCKING A PUNCH
B1	B2	B3

PUSHING BACK	PUNCHING
B4	B5

APPLICATIONS

READY TO ATTACK	BLOCKING	BLOCKING
C1	C2	C3

	BLOCKING	PUNCHING
E1	E2	E3

BLOCKING	BLOCKING & STRIKING	GRABBING
G1	G2	G3

HEIAN GODAN

BLOCKING   **KICKING**   **STRIKING**

D1   D2   D3

JUMPING OVER BO

F1   F2   F3

BLOCKING

F4

BREAKING GRIP

G4

HEIAN GODAN

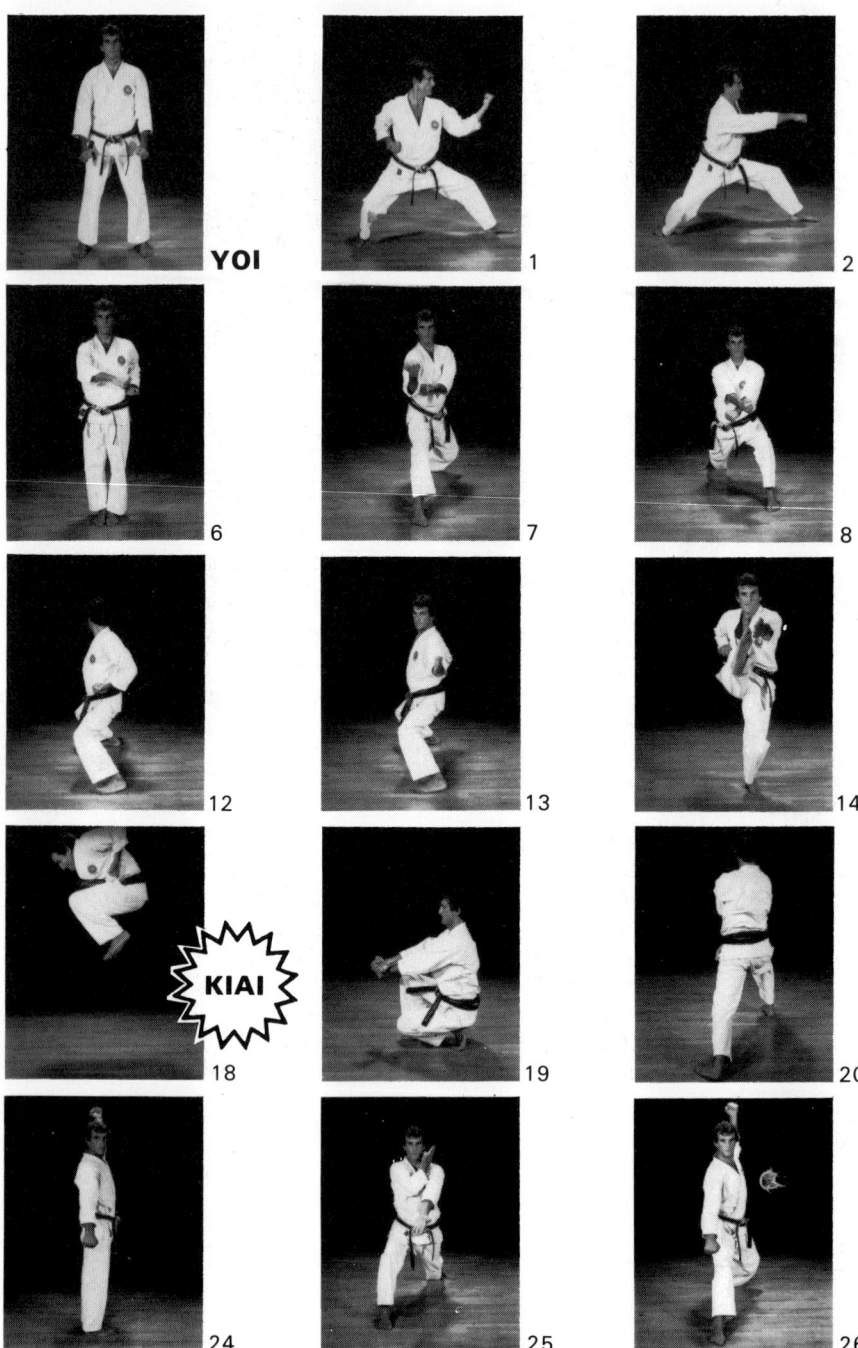

YOI

1

2

6

7

8

12

13

14

KIAI

18

19

20

24

25

26

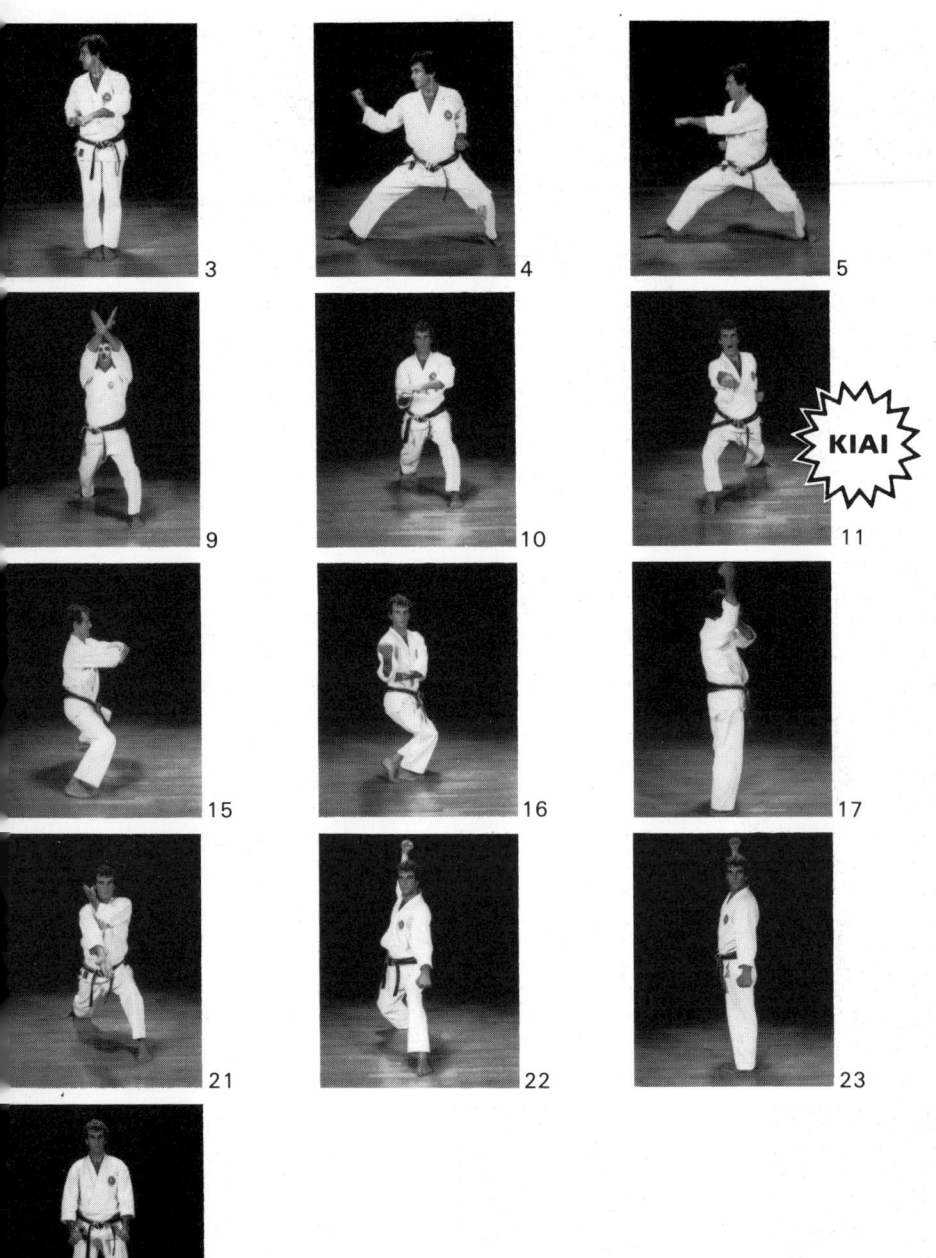

3

4

5

9

10

11 KIAI

15

16

17

21

22

23

YAME

PART 3: KUMITE
SPARRING

The following pages show the step by step method of learning the various types of **Kumite** that eventually lead to **Jiyu Kūmite** (Free Sparring). Each of the four main Kumite constituents are of equal importance and should be practised diligently, for they **all** contain certain aspects not found in any of the others that will subsequently prove to be of enormous benefit.

Simplistically, **Gohon Kumite** teaches formal sparring procedures, whilst **Sambon Kumite** concentrates on dealing with multi-level attacks. In **Kihon Ippon Kumite,** emphasis is placed on **Timing, Distance** and **Focus,** but still very much in a formalised manner. **Jiyū Ippon Kumite** brings the student a step closer to free sparring and ecourages more relaxed, fluid, combination attacks, utilising the evasive techniques of **Tai Sabaki** (Body Shifting).

From an historical viewpoint, both **Funakoshi Sensei** and **Nakayama Sensei** realized many years ago, that if Karate was to gain in popularity and spread worldwide it needed general appeal. Allowing Karate Ka to test their skills against each other in open competition was the obvious way, but both men had **tremendous reservations** as to where this would lead, or indeed, where it would **leave** the Traditional practice of Shotokan Karate-Do.

With hindsight, their decision was the right one, and they have been totally vindicated. Today millions of people of all ages, and from all walks of life, regardless of gender, practice Karate in some form or other. Introducing the competitive aspect into Karate has been the main factor in its phenomenal growth and ironically, the traditionalist element who once feared for the survival of their **"Way of Life"** have become stronger than ever.

As a committed Tradionalist myself, I am very much aware, that a contest, Karate or otherwise, should be concerned with **neither winning nor losing** but instead, **participation.** However, we all know the reality is very different.

Properly organised tournaments are a joy to watch, unfortunately, today, many are an absolute disgrace. Where the **"Sport Element"** is involved, without the ethics of a disciplined "Martial Art" – chaos ensues. Watching victorious contestants prancing around the contest area, waving their fists above their heads, feeding their own ego with thoughts of big purses, large trophies and immortality, leaves most Tradionalists cold and, on occasions like these, it is hard to spot **humility** or the many other attributes the Martial Art inspires.

Jiyū Kumite is a most important part of overall Karate training, but let's get things into perspective – **It's just a part – and no more.**

The moment a Gyaku Zuki scores

GOHON KUMITE
5 ATTACK SPARRING

Gohon Kumite is the first Kumite (Sparring) practice in the Shotokan style. It consists of five singular attacks, stepping forward from the Downward Block position by one participant, and five corresponding defences performed stepping back from the "Yoi" (Ready) position, culminating in a controlled counter attack.

It is designed to develop strong attacks and strong blocks, whilst teaching control on the counter attacks. The beginner will become aware also of timing, distancing and breathing and the basic techniques he has learned so far and practised only in mid air, now take on a new meaning.

With all the techniques pre-arranged, only one **"Kiai"** is necessary on the counter attack.

Two of the most important aspects of **Gohon Kumite** that are often neglected are **Migamae** and **Kigamae**. Both are necessary for attacker and defender alike.

MIGAMAE (Physical Readiness) relates to the technique of Tsuki (Punching), resisting the strongest blocks and Uke (Blocking) the punch regardless of the power.

KIGAMAE involves the mental aspects of both participants, and is concerned with mental attitude, fighting spirit, tenacity, concentration, perserverance and confidence. Everything depends on the efforts of the individual and if both partners practice **Gohon Kumite** equally correctly, then the progress of both will be quite dramatic.

Left: Hidari Jōdan Age Uke

No. 1 JŌDAN

TRAINING METHOD FOR GO HON KUMITE (WITHOUT PARTNER)

STEPPING

START

| YOI | GEDAN BARAI | OI ZUKI | OI ZUKI |

**FROM YOI STEP BACK
INTO GEDAN BARAI**

STEPPING BACK

FINISH

| YOI | RIGHT GYAKU ZUKI | AGE UKE | AGE UKE |

**AFTER GYAKU ZUKI
STEP BACK INTO
YOI POSITION**

FORWARD

FINISH

| OI ZUKI | OI ZUKI | OI ZUKI | YOI |

**AFTER 5TH OI ZUKI
STEP FORWARD INTO
YOI POSITION**

STEPPING BACK

START

| AGE UKE | AGE UKE | AGE UKE | YOI |

No. 2 CHŪDAN

TRAINING METHOD FOR GO HON KUMITE (WITHOUT PARTNER)

STEPPING

START

| YOI | GEDAN BARAI | OI ZUKI | OI ZUKI |

**FROM YOI STEP BACK
INTO GEDAN BARAI**

STEPPING

FINISH

| YOI | GYAKU ZUKI | SOTO UKE | SOTO UKE |

**AFTER GYAKU ZUKI
STEP BACK INTO
YOI POSITION**

FORWARD

OI ZUKI **OI ZUKI** **OI ZUKI** **YOI**

**AFTER 5TH ZUKI
STEP FORWARD INTO
YOI POSITION**

BACK

START

SOTO UKE **SOTO UKE** **SOTO UKE** **YOI**

No. 3 MAE GERI

TRAINING METHOD FOR GO HON KUMITE (WITHOUT PARTNER)

STEPPING

→

START

| YOI | FORWARD STANCE | MAE GERI | MAE GERI |

**FROM YOI STEP
BACK INTO
ZENKUTSU DACHI**

STEPPING

←

FINISH

| YOI | GYAKU ZUKI | GEDAN BARAI | GEDAN BARAI |

**AFTER GYAKU ZUKI
STEP BACK INTO
YOI POSITION**

FINISH

| MAE GERI | MAE GERI | MAE GERI | YOI |

**STEP FORWARD
INTO YOI POSITION**

BACK

START

| GEDAN BARAI | GEDAN BARAI | GEDAN BARAI | YOI |

**FROM YOI POSITION
STEP BACK**

GO HON KUMITE

YOI

ATTACKER STEPS BACK
GEDAN BARAI

MIGI   3   HIDARI
OI ZUKI   AGE UKE

HIDARI   4   MIGI
OI ZUKI   AGE UKE

JŌDAN ATTACK

MIGI	1	HIDARI
OI ZUKI		AGE UKE

HIDARI	2	MIGI
OI ZUKI		AGE UKE

MIGI	5	HIDARI
OI ZUKI		AGE UKE

**COUNTER ATTACK RIGHT
GYAKU ZUKI (KIAI)**

**AFTER, BOTH MOVE IN THIS
DIRECTION ⟶**

213

GO HON KUMITE

YOI

ATTACKER STEPS BACK
GEDAN BARAI

MIGI	3	HIDARI
OI ZUKI		SOTO UDE UKE

HIDARI	4	MIGI SOTO
OI ZUKI		UDE UKE

214

CHŪDAN ATTACK

MIGI OI ZUKI	1	HIDARI SOTO UDE UKE

MIGI OI ZUKI	2	MIGI SOTO UDE UKE

MIGI OI ZUKI	5	HIDARI SOTO UDE UKE

COUNTER ATTACK
CHUDAN GYAKU ZUKI (KIAI)

AFTER, BOTH MOVE IN THIS
DIRECTION ⟶

GO HON KUMITE

YOI

**ATTACKER STEPS BACK
IN ZENKUTSU DACHI**

MIGI   3   **HIDARI**
MAE GERI   **GEDAN BARAI**

HIDARI   4   **MIGI**
MAE GERI   **GEDAN BARAI**

MAE GERI ATTACK

MIGI MAE GERI	1	HIDARI GEDAN BARAI

HIDARI MAE GERI	2	MIGI GEDAN BARAI

MIGI MAE GERI	5	HIDARI GEDAN BARAI

**COUNTER ATTACK WITH
RIGHT GYAKU ZUKI**

**AFTER, BOTH MOVE IN THIS
DIRECTION** ⟶

SAMBON KUMITE
3 LEVEL ATTACK SPARRING

Sambon Kumite or three-attack sparring can be performed in the same way as Go Hon Kumite, with the resulting benefits of developing strong blocks and attacks, together with improvement in "Kime".

On the other hand, Sambon Kumite may take the form of a multi-level sequence so providing pre arranged variation in attack and defence.

On the following pages, the reader will see this form demonstrated in the simple form of Jōdan Oi Zuki, Chūdan Oi Zuki and Chūdan Mae Geri attacks being countered with Age Uke, Soto Ude Uke, Mae Geri and Gyaku Zuki.

Once this simple routine has been perfected, there are no end to the number of hand and foot combinations that can be utilised.

As no attack and defence is usually repeated twice, Sambon Kumite prepares the students' mind for change and encourages him to think quickly.

Shortly he will advance to Kihon Ippon Kumite and its multitude of contrasting techniques, however – firstly he *must* master Sambon Kumite.

Kanazawa Sensei performing his **Special Kata** and about to be attacked by instructors J. van Weenen and M. Randall in a demonstration at Crystal Palace in 1972.

Left: Hidari Chūdan Soto Ude Uke

TRAINING METHOD FOR SAMBON KUMITE (WITHOUT PARTNER)

START

**FROM YOI ATTACKER STEPS
BACK INTO GEDAN BARAI**

1

FINISH

**STEP BACK INTO
YAME POSITION**

2 **STEP FORWARD** 3
INTO YAME POSITION

FROM YOI POSITION
STEP BACK

SAMBON KUMITE

YOI

ATTACKER STEPS BACK
GEDAN BARAI

MAE GERI   3   HIDARI
CHŪDAN   GEDAN BARAI

COUNTER ATTACK
GYAKU ZUKI CHŪDAN

AFTER, BOTH MOVE IN THIS
DIRECTION ⟶

3 LEVEL ATTACK SPARRING

| OI ZUKI JŌDAN | 1 | HIDARI AGE UKE | OI ZUKI CHŪDAN | 2 | MIGI SOTO UDE UKE |

YAME

KIHON IPPON KUMITE
BASIC ONE ATTACK SPARRING

Sometimes called the Basic Kata of Sparring, Kihon Ippon Kumite, or basic 1-attack sparring, allows both persons to take it in turn attacking with pre-arranged techniques and defending and counter attacking.

One learns about "Maai" (Distancing) very early on and the fact that it is not necessary always to defend in straight lines. It is possible to move in other directions and parry the attacker rather than use brute force. Consequently, side stepping and moving at 45° lend themselves admirably for this purpose.

Kihon Ippon Kumite begins with the attacker in Gedan Barai and the defender in the Yoi position. The person defending having completed his counter attack with Kiai, then returns to the Yoi position. He does not pull into the free style "Kamae" pose in any circumstances.

Kihon Ippon Kumite is the formal exercise of sparring and should not be confused with Jiyu Ippon Kumite (semi free 1 attack sparring).

The attacker should attack strongly at all times, exercising control to the face but making some contact if possible when attacking to the mid section.

The defender, after blocking, should focus his counter attack just short of the target and on no account follow through and make contact.

When training in basics in a class situation we always step FORWARD into Gedan Barai. This is to show martial spirit. However, when training with a partner, as in Kihon Ippon Kumite, we always step BACK into Gedan Barai, thus showing humility and gratitude for having someone to train with.

Bowing ("Rei") before training together and after, signifies mutual respect.

Left: Jōdan Shuto Uchi

JŌDAN ATTACKS No. 1

SHIZENTAI 1 **HIDARI GEDAN BARAI**

HIDARI JŌDAN AGE UKE 3 **MIGI JŌDAN OI ZUKI**

HIDARI JŌDAN AGE UKE 2 **MIGI JŌDAN OI ZUKI**
(HALFWAY) **(HALFWAY)**

MIGI CHŪDAN GYAKU ZUKI 4 **MIGI JŌDAN OI ZUKI**

JŌDAN No. 2

SHIZENTAI   1   HIDARI GEDAN BARAI

HIDARI JŌDAN TATE SHUTŌ UKE   3   MIGI JŌDAN OI ZUKI

HIDARI JŌDAN TATE SHUTŌ UKE 2 **MIGI JŌDAN OI ZUKI**
(HALFWAY) **(HALFWAY)**

MIGI JŌDAN SHUTŌ UCHI 4 **MIGI JŌDAN OI ZUKI**

JŌDAN No. 3

SHIZENTAI   1   **HIDARI GEDAN BARAI**

MIGI YOKO GERI KEAGE   3   **MIGI JŌDAN OI ZUKI**

MIGI JŌDAN AGE UKE   2   **MIGI JŌDAN OI ZUKI**
IN HEISOKU DACHI

MIGI CHŪDAN YOKO EMPI   4   **MIGI JŌDAN OI ZUKI**

JŌDAN No. 4

SHIZENTAI   1   **HIDARI GEDAN BARAI**

MIGI CHŪDAN MAWASHI GERI   3   **MIGI JŌDAN OI ZUKI**

HAISHU JŪJI UKE   2   **MIGI JŌDAN OI ZUKI**

HIDARI USHIRO MAWASHI EMPI 4   **MIGI JŌDAN OI ZUKI**

233

CHŪDAN ATTACKS No. 1

SHIZENTAI   1   HIDARI GEDAN BARAI

HIDARI CHŪDAN SOTO UDE UKE   3   MIGI CHŪDAN OI ZUKI

HIDARI CHŪDAN SOTO UDE UKE 2
(HALFWAY)

MIGI CHŪDAN OI ZUKI
(HALFWAY)

MIGI CHŪDAN GYAKU ZUKI 4

MIGI CHŪDAN OI ZUKI

235

CHŪDAN No. 2

SHIZENTAI   1   HIDARI GEDAN BARAI

MIGI CHŪDAN SOTO UDE UKE   3   MIGI CHŪDAN OI ZUKI

MIGI CHŪDAN SOTO UDE UKE 2   **MIGI CHŪDAN OI ZUKI**
(HALFWAY)   **(HALFWAY)**

MIGI CHŪDAN YOKO EMPI   4   **MIGI CHŪDAN OI ZUKI**

CHŪDAN No. 3

SHIZENTAI   1   **HIDARI GEDAN BARAI**

HIDARI JŌDAN KIZAMI ZUKI   3   **MIGI CHŪDAN OI ZUKI**

HIDARI CHŪDAN UCHI UDE UKE 2   **MIGI CHŪDAN OI ZUKI**

MIGI CHŪDAN GYAKU ZUKI   4   **MIGI CHŪDAN OI ZUKI**

CHŪDAN No. 4

SHIZENTAI   1   HIDARI GEDAN BARAI

HIDARI CHŪDAN KIZAMI MAE GERI 3 MIGI CHŪDAN OI ZUKI

HIDARI CHŪDAN SHUTO UKE   2   **MIGI CHŪDAN OI ZUKI**

MIGI CHŪDAN NUKITE   4   **MIGI CHŪDAN OI ZUKI**

241

MAE GERI ATTACKS No. 1

SHIZENTAI   1   HIDARI ZENKUTSU DACHI

HIDARI GEDAN BARAI   3   MIGI CHŪDAN MAE GERI

HIDARI GEDAN BARAI   2   **MIGI CHŪDAN MAE GERI**
(HALFWAY)   **(HALFWAY)**

MIGI CHŪDAN GYAKU ZUKI   4   **MIGI ZENKUTSU DACHI**

MAE GERI No. 2

SHIZENTAI   1   **HIDARI ZENKUTSU DACHI**

HIDARI JŌDAN KIZAMI ZUKI   3

MIGI GEDAN BARAI
GYAKU HANMI

2

MIGI CHŪDAN MAE GERI

MIGI CHŪDAN GYAKU ZUKI

4

MIGI ZENKUTSU DACHI

MAE GERI No. 3

SHIZENTAI   1   HIDARI ZENKUTSU DACHI

PULLING BACK   3   MIGI ZENKUTSU DACHI
(HALFWAY POINT)

GEDAN JŪJI UKE   2   MIGI CHŪDAN MAE GERI

JŌDAN SHUTŌ JUJI UKE   4   MIGI ZENKUTSU DACHI
(A BLOCK USED AS AN ATTACK)

MAE GERI No. 4

SHIZENTAI 1 **HIDARI ZENKUTSU DACHI**

HIDARI CHŪDAN TATE SHUTŌ UKE 3 **MIGI CHŪDAN**
MIGI NEKO ASHI DACHI **MAE GERI SNAPPING BACK**

MIGI GEDAN BARAI 2 **MIGI CHŪDAN MAE GERI**
MIGI NEKO ASHI DACHI

MIGI CHŪDAN MAE EMPI 4

YOKO GERI KEKOMI ATTACKS No.

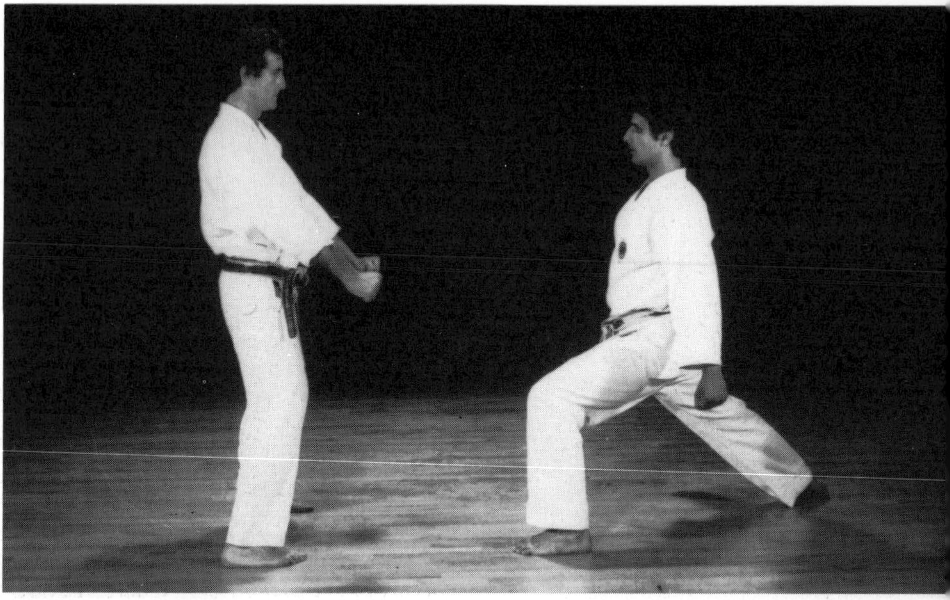

SHIZENTAI 1 HIDARI ZENKUTSU DACHI

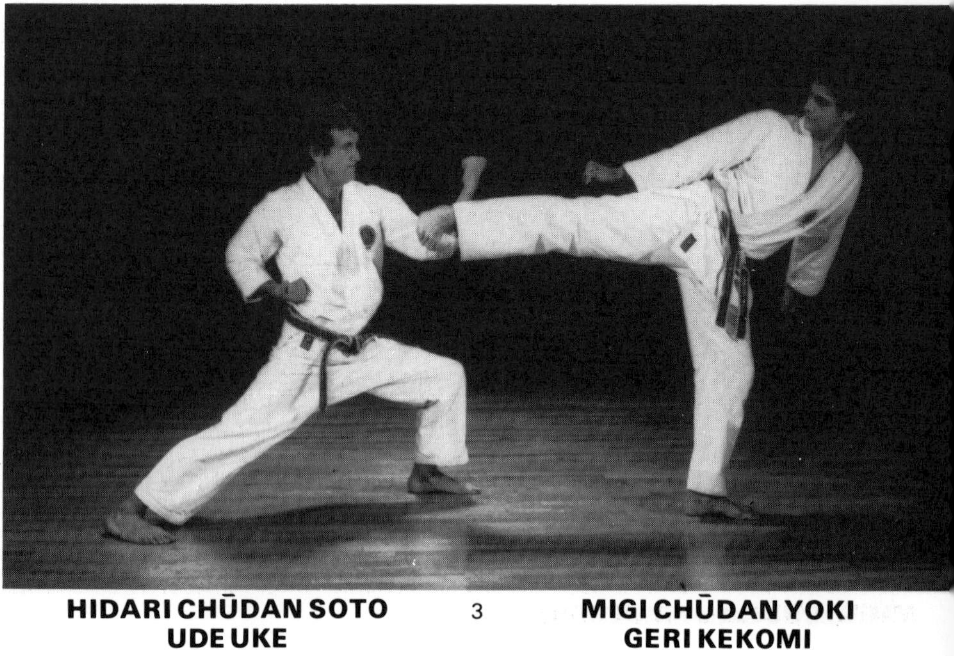

HIDARI CHŪDAN SOTO UDE UKE 3 MIGI CHŪDAN YOKI GERI KEKOMI

HIDARI CHŪDAN SOTO   2   **MIGI CHŪDAN YOKO**
UDE UKE (HALFWAY)   **GERI KEKOMI (HALFWAY)**

MIGI CHŪDAN GYAKU ZUKI   4

KEKOMI No. 2

SHIZENTAI   1   HIDARI ZENKUTSU DACHI

HIDARI GEDAN KAKE UKE   3   MIGI CHŪDAN YOKO GERI KEKOMI

HIDARI GEDAN KAKE UKE   2   **MIGI CHŪDAN YOKO**
(HALFWAY)   **GERI KEKOMI (HALFWAY)**

MIGI JŌDAN HAITO UCHI   4

MAWASHI GERI ATTACKS No. 1

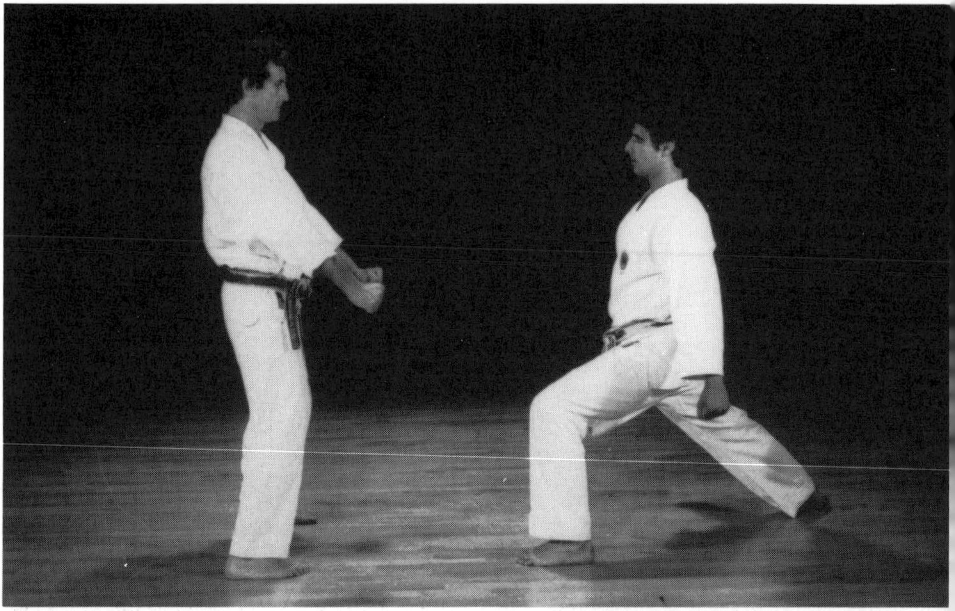

1 **HIDARI ZENKUTSU DACHI**

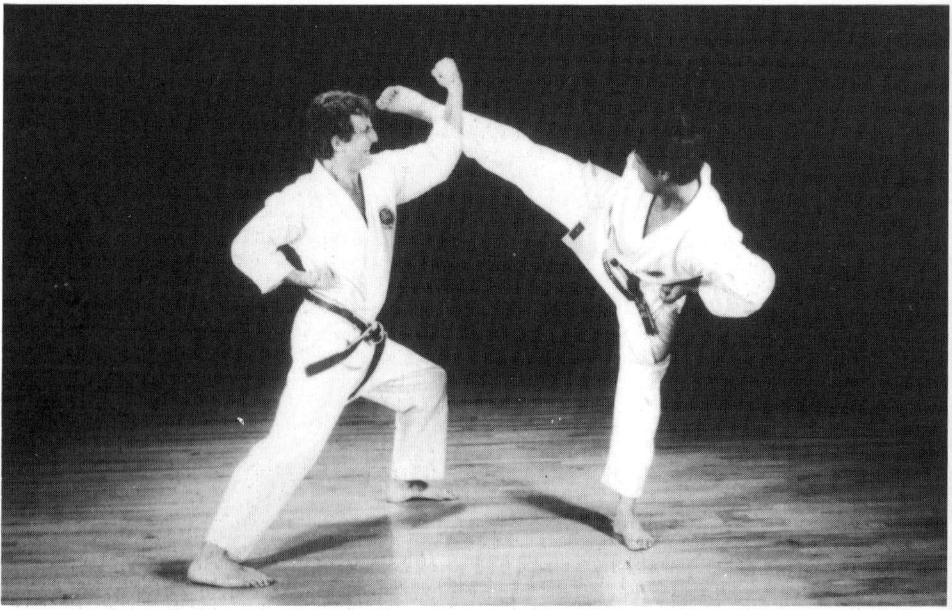

HIDARI JŌDAN UCHI UDE UKE 3 **MIGI JŌDAN MAWASHI GERI**

HIDARI JŌDAN UCHI UDE UKE 2 **MIGI JŌDAN MAWASHI GERI**
(HALFWAY) **(HALFWAY)**

MIGI CHŪDAN GYAKU ZUKI 4

MAWASHI GERI No. 2

1   HIDARI ZENKUTSU DACHI

MIGI JŌDAN MAWASHI GERI   3   JŌDAN SHUTŌ MOROTE UKE

JŌDAN SHUTŌ MOROTE UKE   2   **MIGI JŌDAN MAWASHI GERI**
(HALFWAY)   **(HALFWAY)**

MIGI CHŪDAN MOROTE YOKO EMPI   4

KIHON IPPON KUMITE. SET 5

Set 5 consists of 5 attacks. One Jōdan Oi Zuki, one Chūdan Oi Zuki, one Chūdan Mae Geri, one Chūdan Yoko Geri Kekomi and one Jōdan Mawashi Geri, together with five designated defences and counter attacks.

DEFENCES

JŌDAN ATTACK No. 5 DEFENCE

| SHIZENTAI/
NATURAL
STANCE. | HIDARI GEDAN BARAI/
LEFT DOWNWARD
BLOCK (FORWARD
STANCE). | HIDARI JŌDAN AGE
UKE/
LEFT UPPER RISING
BLOCK (FORWARD
STANCE). | MIGI JŌDAN
OI ZUKI/
RIGHT UPPER
STEPPING PUNCH
(FORWARD STANCE |

CHŪDAN ATTACK No. 5 DEFENCE

| SHIZENTAI/
NATURAL
STANCE. | HIDARI GEDAN BARAI/
LEFT DOWNWARD
BLOCK (FORWARD
STANCE). | HIDARI CHŪDAN EMPI
UKE/
LEFT MIDDLE ELBOW
BLOCK (STRADDLE
STANCE). | MIGI CHŪDAN OI ZU
RIGHT MIDDLE
STEPPING PUNCH
(FORWARD STANCE |

Originally, the Beginners Guide to Shotokan Karate was produced as a working manual to assist the student in the fundamentals of the style, as taught by his own instructor. Almost a decade later it has become **The Beginners Text Book** and is sold in most English speaking countries and surprisingly enough, in Japan too.

Omitted in previous editions but now included is Kihon Ippon Kumite Set 5. This is the last *formal* set in Shotokan but numerous other techniques of Kihon Ippon Kumite are practised on an individual basis.

As the student approaches Set 5, his understanding of *Sabaki* (Stepping and Dodging) should have improved. Techniques should now be performed correctly, with good posture and proper breathing. *Zanshin* (Awareness) should be keener and *Yomi* (Perceptivity) playing an almost intuitive role.

Throughout the practice of Kihon Ippon Kumite, Sahō (Etiquette) should prevail, despite the students degree of tiredness. Finally, as with previous Kumite, briefly maintain the focus (Kime) of the final counter attack. This will enable the correct muscles to be tensed and developed accordingly.

BEFORE MAE GERI, PULL LEFT FOOT BACK 1/2 STEP FOR CORRECT DISTANCING.

MIGI JŌDAN MAE GERI/ RIGHT UPPER FRONT KICK.

MIGI JŌDAN OI ZUKI/ RIGHT UPPER STEPPING PUNCH (FORWARD STANCE).

MIGI TATE EMPI UCHI/ RIGHT (VERTICAL) UPPER RISING ELBOW STRIKE (FORWARD STANCE).

MIGI JŌDAN OI ZUKI/ RIGHT UPPER STEPPING PUNCH (FORWARD STANCE).

HALF-WAY POSITION TO USHIRO MAWASHI EMPI UCHI.

MIGI JŌDAN USHIRO MAWASHI EMPI UCHI/ RIGHT UPPER REVERSE (BACK) ROUNDHOUSE ELBOW STRIKE (STRADDLE STANCE).

MIGI CHŪDAN OI ZUKI/ RIGHT MIDDLE STEPPING PUNCH (FORWARD STANCE).

MAE GERI ATTACK No. 5 DEFENCE

**SHIZENTAI/
NATURAL STANCE.**
**HIDARI ZENKUTSU
DACHI/
LEFT FORWARD
STANCE.**
**HALFWAY POSITION TO HIDARI
SUKUI UKE.**

YOKO GERI KEKOMI ATTACK No. 3 DEFENCE

**SHIZENTAI/
NATURAL STANCE.**
**HIDARI ZENKUTSU
DACHI/
LEFT FORWARD
STANCE.**
**MIGI USHIRO GEDAN
BARAI/
RIGHT BACK
DOWNWARD BLOCK IN
FORWARD STANCE.**
**MIGI CHŪDAN YOKO
GERI KEKOMI/
RIGHT MIDDLE SIDE
THRUST KICK.**

MAWASHI GERI ATTACK No. 3 DEFENCE

**SHIZENTAI/
NATURAL STANCE.**
**HIDARI ZENKUTSU
DACHI/
LEFT FORWARD
STANCE**
**MIGI JŌDAN SOTO UDE
UKE IN KIBA DACHI/
RIGHT UPPER OUTSIDE
FOREARM BLOCK IN
STRADDLE STANCE.**
**MIGI JŌDAN
MAWASHI GERI/
RIGHT UPPER
ROUNDHOUSE KICK.**

HIDARI SUKUI UKE IN KŌKUTSU DACHI/ LEFT SCOOPING BLOCK IN BACK STANCE

MIGI CHUDAN MAE GERI/ RIGHT MIDDLE FRONT KICK

MIGI CHŪDAN GYAKU ZUKI/ RIGHT MIDDLE REVERSE PUNCH IN FORWARD STANCE

MIGI ZENKUTSU DACHI/ RIGHT FORWARD STANCE

MIGI CHŪDAN YOKO GERI KEKOMI/ RIGHT MIDDLE SIDE THRUST KICK.

MIGI ZENKUTSU DACHI/ RIGHT FORWARD STANCE.

MIGI CHŪDAN YOKO EMPI UCHI IN KIBA DACHI/ RIGHT MIDDLE SIDE ELBOW STRIKE IN STRADDLE STANCE.

MIGI ZENKUTSU DACHI/ RIGHT FORWARD STANCE.

MIGI CHŪDAN MAE KIZAMI GERI/ RIGHT MIDDLE FRONT LEG SNAPPING KICK.

MIGI ZENKUTSU DACHI/ RIGHT FORWARD STANCE.

HIDARI CHŪDAN GYAKU ZUKI/ LEFT MIDDLE REVERSE PUNCH IN FORWARD STANCE.

MIGI ZENKUTSU DACHI/ RIGHT FORWARD STANCE.

261

KIHON IPPON KUMITE – COMPULSORY DEFENCES
All defences listed below are against a right hand or foot attack

SET 1
Attacks: Jōdan/Chūdan/Mae-geri (one of each, right and left)

Defences:
Jōdan No. 1   Hidari-jōdan age-uke/Migi-chūdan, gyaku-zuki
Chūdan No. 1   Hidari-chūdan soto-ude-uke/Migi-chūdan, gyaku-zuki
Mae-geri No. 1   Hidari-gedan-barai/Migi-chūdan Gyaku-zuki

SET 2
Attacks: Jōdan/Chūdan/Mae-geri (one of each, right and left)

Defences:
Jōdan No.2   Hidari-jōdan-tate shutō-uke/Migi-jōdan, shutō-uchi
Chūdan No. 2   Migi-chūdan, soto-ude-uke/Migi-chūdan, yoko-enpi-uchi
Mae-geri No. 2   Migi-gyaku gedan-barai/Hidari-jōdan, kizami-zuki/
                             Migi-chūdan gyaku-zuki

SET 3
Attacks: Jōdan/Chūdan/Mae-geri/Kekomi/Mawashi-geri
                             (one of each, right and left)

Defences:
Jōdan No. 3   Migi-jōdan age-uke/Migi-yoko-geri keage/Migi-chūdan
                             yoko-enpi-uchi
Chūdan No. 3   Hidari-chūdan uchi-ude-uke/Hidari-jōdan, kizami-zuki/
                             Migi-chūdan gyaku-zuki
Mae-geri No. 3   Migi-gedan juji-uke/Jōdan-shutō, juji-uchi
Kekomi No. 1   Hidari-chūdan soto-ude-uke/Migi-chūdan, gyaku-zuki
Mawashi-geri No. 1   Hidari-haiwan uchi-uke/Migi-chūdan, gyaku-zuki

SET 4
Attacks: Same as Set 3

Defences:
Jōdan No. 4   Hidari-jōdan haishu, juji-uke/Chūdan mawashi-geri/
                             Hidari-jōdan ushiro, mawashi, enpi
Chūdan No. 4   Hidari-chūdan shutō-uke/Kizami, mae-geri/Migi-
                             chūdan-tate yonhon-nukite
Mae-geri No. 4   Migi-gedan-barai/Hidari-gyaku-tate, shutō-uke/Migi-
                             chūdan, mae-enpi
Kekomi No. 2   Hidari-chūdan kake-uke/Migi-jōdan haito-uchi
Mawashi-geri No. 2   Tate-heiko shutō-uke/Soete-yoko, enpi-uchi

SET 5
Attacks: Same as Set 3

Defences:
Jōdan No. 5   Hidari-jōdan age-uke/Migi-jōdan, mae-geri/Migi-jōdan,
                             enpi-uchi
Chūdan No. 5   Hidari-chūdan enpi-uke/Migi-jōdan, ushiro, mawashi,
                             enpi-uchi
Mae-geri No. 5   Hidari-chūdan sukui-uke/Migi-chūdan, gyaku-zuki
Kekomi No. 3   Migi-ushiro gedan-barai/Migi-chudan yoko-geri,
                             Kekomi/Migi-yoko, enpi
Mawashi-geri No. 3   Migi-jōdan, soto-ude-uke/Mae-kizami-geri, Hidari-
                             gyaku-zuki

Grand Master **Fusajiro Takagi** 8th dan with the author on the occasion of the first Japan Karate Masters Seminar held at Shiga in 1985. John also had the honour of training under the great **Manzo Iwata** of Shito Ryu, who sadly is no longer with us.

1971 and **Kanazawa Sensei** steps inside John van Weenen's Oi Zuki and Counters with Ushiro Mawashi Geri

JIYŪ IPPON KUMITE
SEMI FREE
ONE ATTACK SPARRING

Jiyū Ippon Kumite is the transitional stage between **Kihon Ippon Kumite** and **Jiyū Kumite.** Up until now, in all the various forms of Kumite practises, the methods of attack, defence and counter attack have all been pre-arranged and the overriding theme running through them all is one of formality. In changing to a more informal fighting style, many students of Shotokan experience a degree of difficulty, but with practice, this is soon overcome.

For **Jiyū Ippon Kumite** both participants adopt *"Jiyū Dachi"* (Free Fighting Stance) bringing both fists up in front of their body for protection. Only the attack is pre-arranged and the defence and counter attack are of the defenders own choice, after which, he returns to **Jiyū Dachi,** or in some cases **Hikite Gamae.**

This type of Kumite encourages a much more relaxed, fluid exchange and requires the defender to think for himself rather than following an instruction. **Timing** is vital, especially for the attacker and distancing important for both attacker and defender.

Practising **Tai Sabaki** (Body Shifting) allows the defender to move in virtually any direction to block, dodge, parry, sweep or evade the attack before counter attacking himself. These counter attacks often take the form of multiple attacks utilising a combination of moves. Using hands and feet alternatively to counter attack at different levels, invariably ensures a successful outcome.

In **Jiyū Ippon Kumite,** by taking advantage of your opponents strength and speed, it is possible to increase or even double the power of your own counter attack.

By watching your opponents **breathing** and attacking whilst he is **inhaling** adds significantly to your chances of success.

JIYŪ IPPON KUMITE: SET 1

JŌDAN ATTACK

JIYŪ GAMAE

JŌDAN TATE SHUTŌ UKE

JŌDAN Using the front foot as a pivot, step back with the r foot (right) 45° to the right, TATE SHUTŌ UKE, preferably against the crook of the arm.

CHŪDAN ATTACK

JIYŪ GAMAE

CHŪDAN SOTO UDE UKE

CHŪDAN Using the left foot as a pivot, step back to the left v the rear foot 45° using a quick rotation of the hips CHŪDAN SOTO UDE UKE. Use the reaction, GYAK ZUKI.

MAE GERI ATTACK

JIYŪ GAMAE

GEDAN BARAI

MAE GERI Using the front foot as a pivot, step back to the righ the back foot (right) 45° GEDAN BARAI. Execute GYAKU ZUKI by taking advantage of the impulse of t MAE GERI against the hand and the opposition of th

KIAI

3

HIKITE GAMAE

CHŪDAN GYAKU ZUKI (KIAI)
Use the reaction, GYAKU ZUKI. Simultaneously pull
back the fist and the front foot a half step to assume
the stance HANMI SHIZENTAI, HIKITE GAMAE.

4

KIAI

3

4

CHŪDAN GYAKU ZUKI (KIAI)

HIKITE GAMAE

KIAI

3

4

CHŪDAN GYAKU ZUKI (KIAI)
rear leg on the floor. The retreating movement
(TENSHIN, TAI SABAKI) is identical to JŌDAN OI
ZUKI No. 1.

HIKITE GAMAE

ATTACKER: MAC ROOME
DEFENDER: CHRIS BURTON

JIYŪ IPPON KUMITE: SET 2

JŌDAN ATTACK

JIYŪ GAMAE

KIAI

JŌDAN NAGASHI UKE DOJI CHŪDAN URA ZUKI (KIAI)

JŌDAN Step forward with the front foot (left). At the same time NAGASHI UKE, URA ZUKI. Move the rear foot 45° to the left as you thrust away the opponent with the left hand (The one using NAGASHI UKE).

HIDARI SEIRYUTŌ GEDAN UKE

KIAI

JŌDAN URAKEN UCHI. (KIAI)

CHŪDAN Using the rear foot (right) as a pivot, yield to the attack by stepping backwards in a straight line, HIDARI SEIRYUTŌ GEDAN UKE bringing the right fist on the left shoulder. Take advantage of the simultaneous and combined action of the two joints: left knee and right elbow to execute URAKEN UCHI.

MIGI GEDAN BARAI

HIKITE

MAE GERI Using the rear foot as a pivot, step back to the rear left with the front foot (left) 45° GEDAN BARAI in MIGI ZENKUTSU DACHI. Simultaneously, withdraw the front foot one step, pulling the right fist back to the hip and thrusting away the left hand shaped as in TATE SHUTŌ. Spring forward to the outside of the

CHUDAN ATTACK

JIYŪ GAMAE — **1**

END OF JŌDAN

3 — HIKITE GAMAE

MAE GERI ATTACK

JIYŪ GAMAE — **1**

END OF CHŪDAN

4 — HIKITE GAMAE

KIAI

4 — JŌDAN JUN ZUKI (KIAI)

opponent, CHOKU ZUKI (right fist) using the antagonistic muscles of the rear leg: First the flexor, then the extensor.

5 — HIKITE GAMAE

END OF MAE GERI

ATTACKER: KEVIN STARK
DEFENDER: ALAN BRISTOW

JIYŪ IPPON KUMITE: SET 3

JŌDAN ATTACK

JIYŪ GAMAE

JŌDAN AGE UKE

HIKITE GAMAE

E
N
D

O
F

J
Ō
D
A
N

JŌDAN

Using the rear foot (right) as a pivot, step back quick with the front foot 45° to the rear left, JŌDAN AGE UKE in MIGI ZENKUTSU DACHI, then KIZAMI MAWASHI GERI, GYAKU ZUKI.

HIKITE GAMAE

SIDE VIEW OF NO 2

KIZAMI MAWASHI GERI

HIDARI CHŪDAN, GYAKU ZUKI (KIAI)

ŪDAN ATTACK

JIYŪ GAMAE

HIDARI GYAKU ZUKI (KIAI)

SIDE VIEW OF NO 3

E
N
D

O
F

C
H
Ū
D
A
N

CHŪDAN

Using the rear foot (right) as a pivot, execute, at the same time, a TAI SABAKI (change of direction) and GYAKU ZUKI without blocking, by moving the front foot (left) 90° to the left.

ATTACKER: AZAD KUMAR
DEFENDER: LESLIE ALBONE

JIYŪ IPPON KUMITE: SET 3

MAE GERI ATTACK

JIYŪ GAMAE

YOKO KEKOMI ATTACK

JIYŪ GAMAE

MAWASHI GERI ATTACK

JIYŪ GAMAE

GEDAN JŪJI UKE

MAE GERI
Step forward with the front (left) GEDAN JŪJI UKE (the left wrist over the right), simultaneously, move t rear foot 45° to the left TENSHIN and YOKO SHUT UCHI. The distribution of the blocking force is 7:3 (right:left)

HIDARI CHŪDAN SOTO UDE UKE

YOKO KEKOMI
Using the left foot as a pivot, step back to the left 4 with the rear foot, using a quick rotation of the hips CHŪDAN SOTO UDE UKE. Use the reaction, GYAK ZUKI. This technique is identical to OI ZUKI CHŪDA NO 1.

JŌDAN HAIWAN UKE

MAWASHI GERI
Using the front foot as a pivot, TENSHIN, by movin 90° to the right the rear foot (right) and at the same time execute, HAIWAN UKE, GYAKU ZUKI.

YOKO SHUTŌ UCHI (KIAI)

HIKITE GAMAE

END OF MAE GERI

MIGI CHŪDAN GYAKU ZUKI (KIAI)

HIKITE GAMAE

END OF YOKO KEKOMI

MIGI CHŪDAN GYAKU ZUKI (KIAI)

HIKITE GAMAE

END OF MAWASHI GERI

ATTACKER: AZAD KUMAR
DEFENDER: LESLIE ALBONE

JIYŪ IPPON KUMITE: SET 4

JŌDAN ATTACK

1 JIYŪ GAMAE

2 HIRATE BARAI

JŌDAN Step forward 45° to the left with the front foot, HIRATE BARAI, TEISHŌ UCHI. Using the left foot as a pivot, move the right foot 135° (TENSHIN) to the left

CHŪDAN ATTACK

5 FRONT VIEW OF NO 4

E
N
D

O F

J
Ō
D
A
N

1 JIYŪ GAMAE

CHŪDAN MAE GERI, of encounter (DEAÏ): before the opponent executes 3/4 of UNSOKU. Execute GEDAN BARAI at the same time the front foot is back to the rear right and resume the guard. Jump forward, JŌDAN KIZAMI ZUKI.

4 KAMAE-JIYŪ DACHI

KIAI

5 HIDARI JŌDAN KIZAMI ZUKI (KIAI)

MIGI CHŪDAN TEISHO UCHI (KIAI)

HIKITE GAMAE

DEAI MIGI CHUDAN MAE GERI (KIAI)

HIDARI GEDAN BARAI

MAE GERI ATTACK

HIKITE GAMAE

END OF CHŪDAN

JIYŪ GAMAE

ATTACKER: CHRIS BURTON
DEFENDER: DONOVAN SLUE

JIYŪ IPPON KUMITE: SET 4

MAE GERI ATTACK

GEDAN OSAE UKE

MIGI NAGASHI UKE

MAE GERI Using the front foot (left) as a pivot, spring forward to the left, blocking with OSAE UKE changing to NAGASHI UKE. Rotate 180°, MIGI GYAKU ZUKI.

YOKO KEKOMI ATTACK

JIYŪ GAMAE

AWASE SEIRYUTŌ UKE

YOKO KEKOMI Using the rear foot as a pivot, step back to the rear right 45° with the front foot (left). AWASE SEIRYUTŌ UKE, the edge of the right hand crossed over

MAWASHI GERI ATTACK

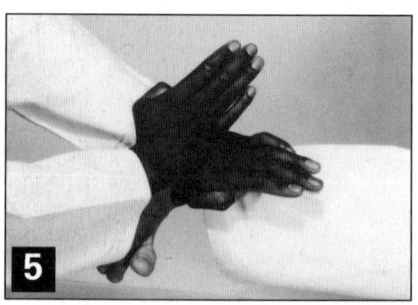

CLOSE UP OF HANDS WHEN BLOCKING

E
N
D

O
F

Y
O
K
O

K
E
K
O
M
I

JIYŪ GAMAE

MAWASHI GERI Using the front foot (left) as a pivot, spring forward KIZAMI GYAKU ZUKI. Immediately thrust the opponent away with the right hand shaped as in TATE SHUTŌ on the neck or the shoulder and move the left foot to the right.

SEMI FREE
ONE ATTACK SPARRING

MIGI CHŪDAŇ GYAKU ZUKI (KIAI)

END OF MAE GERI

HIKITE GAMAE

JŌDAN TATE ZUKI (KIAI)

...he left wrist, the finger tips pointing towards the face of the opponent. TATE ZUKI is executed by the simultaneous and instantaneous extensions of the left knee and right elbow.

HIKITE GAMAE

JŌDAN KIZAMI GYAKU ZUKI (KIAI)

END OF MAWASHI GERI

HIKITE GAMAE

ATTACKER: CHRIS BURTON
DEFENDER: DONOVAN SLUE

277

JIYŪ IPPON KUMITE: SET 5

JODAN ATTACK

JIYŪ GAMAE

KIAI

JŌDAN OTOSHI UKE DŌJI TOBI MAE GERI URAKEN UCHI (KIAI)

| **JŌDAN** | Bring the front foot (left) closer, at the same time, OSAE UKE with the palm of the left hand and jump with the right foot, MIGI ASHI TOBI GERI, URA KEN UCHI. |

GYAKU GEDAN BARAI

JŌDAN USHIRO MAWASHI GERI

| **CHŪDAN** | Step forward with the left foot to the front left GYAKU GEDAN BARAI JŌDAN USHIRO MAWASHI GERI. Follow up as you reap his front leg with a |

UKE GAESHI

KIAI

MIGI GYAKU ZUKI (KIAI)

JIYŪ GAMAE **1**

E N D   O F   J Ō D A N

HIKITE GAMAE **3**

ŌSOTO GARI (COMMENCING) **4**
throwing technique similar to ŌSOTOGARI in JUDŌ.
Release his hand by striking with the edge of the left
hand and execute GYAKU ZUKI downwards.

ŌSOTO GARI (COMPLETING) **5**

MAE GERI ATTACK

JIYŪ GAMAE **1**

E N D   O F   C H Ū D A N

HIKITE GAMAE **8**

ATTACKER: LESLIE ALBONE
DEFENDER: MICHAEL BATTEN

JIYŪ IPPON KUMITE: SET 5

MAE GERI ATTACK CONTINUED

MIGI GEDAN BARAI

HIDARI GYAKU TATE SHUTŌ

MAE GERI — Step back and 45° to the left, blocking with a right downward block and immediately execute a left reverse vertical knife hand block as you withdraw the right foot back one foot length.

YOKO KEKOMI ATTACK

HIKITE GAMAE

E N D   O F   M A E   G E R I

JIYŪ GAMAE

MAWASHI GERI ATTACK

E N D   O F   Y O K O   K E K O M I

HIKITE GAMAE

JIYŪ GAMAE

MAWASHI GERI — Using the rear foot as a pivot, step back with the front foot (left) simultaneously blocking with AWASE SHUTŌ UKE AND MAWASHI GERI with the right foot

HIDARI ASHI BARAI
With your left leg sweep his front leg and quickly follow up with a reverse punch - pull back into HIKITE GAMAE.

MIGI GYAKU ZUKI (KIAI)

HIDARI KAKE UKE (HAIWAN)
Using the front foot as a pivot, HIDARI HAIWAN UKE. Quickly, step forward from the outside with the right foot. USHIRO MAWASHI ENPI in ZENKUTSU DACHI. Eliminate every unnecessary movement between UKE and UCHI.

YOKO KEKOMI

USHIRO MAWASHI ENPI (KIAI)

AWASE SHUTÔ UKE DÔJI JÔDAN KIZAMI MAWASHI GERI (KIAI)

HIKITE GAMAE

END OF MAWASHI GERI

ATTACKER: LESLIE ALBONE
DEFENDER: MICHAEL BATTEN

JIYŪ IPPON KUMITE: USHIR

No. 1 DEFENCE

JIYŪ GAMAE

GYAKU SUKUI UKE

No.1 DEFENCE	Using the rear foot as a pivot, move 45° to the rear right the front foot (left) with a hip rotation, GYAKU SUKUI UKE, MAWASHI ZUKI.

No. 2 DEFENCE

JIYŪ GAMAE

MAE UDE SUKUI UKE

No.2 DEFENCE	Simultaneously, spring forward with the front foot (left) towards the opponent's supporting leg, GYAKU UDE UKE. In KIBADACHI, lift and throw, to the floor, HIDARI ASHI BARAI SUKUI NAGE. Finish with GYAKI ZUKI.

No. 3 DEFENCE

JIYŪ GAMAE

SUKUI UKE

No.3 DEFENCE	Using the rear foot as a pivot, simultaneously, step back with the front foot (left) MIGITE SUKUI UKE-HIDARI USHIRO GERI by turning counter clockwise.

GERI ATTACK

3 JODAN MAWASHI ZUKI (KIAI)

4 HIKITE GAMAE

END OF No.1 DEFENCE

3 DŌJI ASHIBARAI SUKUI NAGE

4 GYAKU ZUKI (KIAI)   HIKITE GAMAE

END OF No.2 DEFENCE

3 HIDARI USHIRO GERI (KIAI)

4 ZANSHIN GAMAE

END OF No.3 DEFENCE

ATTACKER: MICHAEL BATTEN
DEFENDER: LESLIE ALBONE

JIYŪ IPPON KUMITE: JŌDAN KIZAMI

No. 1 DEFENCE

JIYŪ GAMAE

JŌDAN URAKEN UCHI (KIAI)

No.1 DEFENCE Using the rear foot as a pivot, step forward 45° to the left with the front foot (left). JŌDAN URAKEN UCHI in ZENKUTSU DACHI. Follow-up immediately with HIDARI GYAKU ZUKI in MIGI ZENKUTSU DACHI with a quick hip rotation.

No. 2 DEFENCE

HIKITE GAMAE

END OF No.1 DEFENCE

JIYŪ GAMAE

No.2 DEFENCE Execute simultaneously, ASHI BARAI and JŌDAN HARAI UKE, then URA ZUKI when the foot touches the floor. Immediately thrust the opponent away with the palm heel of the hand on the shoulder.

No. 3 DEFENCE

HIKITE GAMAE

END OF No.2 DEFENCE

JIYŪ GAMAE

ZUKI ATTACK

3

HIKITE GAMAE (SNAPPING ARM BACK WHILE MOVING OUT)

KIAI

4

CHÛDAN GYAKU ZUKI

2

JÔDAN HIRATE HARAI UKE DÔJI ASHIBARAI

KIAI

3

CHÛDAN URA ZUKI (KIAI)

KIAI

2

HAIWAN NAGASHI UKE DÔJI URAKEN UCHI (KIAI)
As pictured here JÔDAN URA ZUKI may be used as an alternative to URAKEN.

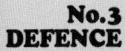

No.3 DEFENCE Using the rear foot as a pivot, simultaneously step forward with the front foot (left) HAIWAN NAGASHI UKE, URAKEN UCHI in FUDÔ DACHI. Step away immediately.

3

HIKITE GAMAE

END OF No.3 DEFENCE

ATTACKER: MICHAEL BATTEN
DEFENDER: JOHN VAN WEENEN

285

JIYŪ IPPON KUMITE: CHŪDAN GYAKU

No. 1 DEFENCE

JIYŪ GAMAE

HIDARI JŌDAN KIZAMI ZUKI

TSUKI HANASHI GAMAE

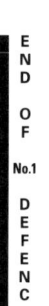

END OF No.1 DEFENCE

No. 2 DEFENCE

JIYŪ GAMAE

HIKITE

END OF No.2 DEFENCE

No. 3 DEFENCE

JIYŪ GAMAE

SEMI FREE
ONE ATTACK SPARRING

KAMAE

MIGI CHŪDAN GYAKU ZUKI (KIAI)

No.1 DEFENCE Using the front foot as a pivot, move 45° to the left the rear foot (right) JŌDAN KIZAMI ZUKI, quickly pulling the elbow close to the hip, then, GYAKU ZUKI.

GEDAN BARAI, DŌJI CHŪDAN MAWASHI GERI.

HEIKŌ USHIRO SHUTŌ UCHI (KIAI)

No.2 DEFENCE Execute GEDAN BARAI-MAWASHI GERI, simultaneously as you step forward with the left foot outside the opponent's left foot. Spring forward, HEIKŌ USHIRO SHUTŌ UCHI as the left leg is straightened.

HIDARI GEDAN BARAI

HIDARI JŌDAN URAKEN UCHI (KIAI)   **HIKITE GAMAE.**

END OF No.3 DEFENCE

No.3 DEFENCE GEDAN BARAI as you move the right foot, then, with the same hand, URAKEN UCHI.

ATTACKER: MICHAEL BATTEN
DEFENDER: JOHN VAN WEENEN

JIYU IPPON KUMITE – COMPULSORY DEFENCES
All defences listed below are against a right hand or foot attack

SET 1
Attacks: Jōdan/Chūdan/Mae-geri (one of each, right only)
Defences:
Jōdan No. 1   Hidari-jōdan-tate shutō-uke/Migi-chūdan gyaku-zuki/Hikite-gamae
Chūdan No. 1   Hidari-chūdan soto-ude-uke/Migi-chūdan, gyaku-zuki/Hikite-gamae
Mae-geri No. 1   Hidari-gedan-barai/Migi-chūdan gyaku-zuki/Hikite-gamae

SET 2
Attacks: Jōdan/Chūdan/Mae-geri (one of each, right and left)
Defences:
Jōdan No.2   Hidari-jōdan nagashi-uke/Migi-chūdan ura-zuki/Hikite-gamae
Chūdan No. 2   Hidari-seiryuto gedan-uke/Migi-jōdan uraken-uchi/Hikite-gamae
Mae-geri No. 2   Migi-gedan-barai/Hidari-gyaku, tate-shutō/Migi-jōdan choku-zuki/Hikite-gamae

SET 3
Attacks: Jōdan/Chūdan/Mae-geri/Kekomi/Mawashi-geri (one of each, right and left)
Defences:
Jōdan No. 3   Migi-jōdan, age-uke/Migi-kizami, mawashi-geri/Hidari-chūdan gyaku-zuki/Hikite-gamae
Chūdan No. 3   Hidari-gyaku-zuki/Hikite-gamae
Mae-geri No. 3   Hidari-gedan juji-uke/Hidari-yoko, shutō-uchi/Hikite-gamae
Kekomi No. 1   Hidari soto-ude-uke/Migi-chudan gyaku-zuki/Hikite-gamae
Mawashi-geri No. 1   Hidari-jōdan haiwan-uke/Migi-chūdan, gyaku-zuki/Hikite-gamae

SET 4
Attacks: Same as Set 3
Defences:
Jōdan No. 4   Hidari-hirate-barai/Migi-teisho-uchi/Hikite-barai
Chūdan No. 4   Migi-chūdan mae-geri/Hidari-gedan-barai/Kamae/Hidari-jōdan kizami-zuki, Zanshin-gamae
Mae-geri No. 4   Migi-gedan-osae nagashi-uke/Hidari-chūdan gyaku-zuki/Hikite-gamae
Kekomi No. 2   Awase-seiryuto-uke/Migi-jōdan tate-zuki/Zanshin-gamae
Mawashi-geri No. 2   Hidari-jōdan-kizami gyaku-zuki/Migi-tate shutō-uke

SET 5
Attacks: Same as Set 3
Defences:
Jōdan No. 5   Hidari-osae-uke/Migi-tobi-geri/Uraken-uchi
Chūdan No. 5   Migi-gyaku gedan-barai/Migi-jōdan-ushiro mawashi-geri/Migi-ashi-barai/Migi-gyaku-zuki/Hikite-gamae
Mae-geri No. 5   Migi-gedan-barai/Hidari-gyaku tate-shutō/Hidari-ashi-barai/Migi-gyaku-zuki/Hikite-gamae
Kekomi No. 3   Hidari-kake-uke (Haiwan)/Ushiro-mawashi, enpi/Zanshin-gamae
Mawashi-geri No. 3   Awase-shuto-uke and Migi-jodan-kizami mawashi-geri

Kanazawa Sensei performing "Yoko Tobi Geri"

289

PART 4
KARATE FOR
EVERYONE

WOMEN IN KARATE SELF DEFENCE

Just as we have seen a huge increase in the number of children taking up Karate, so too has the number of women being attracted to the art increased. Twenty-five years ago, women made up about **2%** of the total class, whereas today, that figure is nearer **20%**. The reasons for this are not difficult to understand.

Year by year there has been a disturbing increase in crimes of violence. Rape has become widespread, so much so that "rape within the confines of marriage" has become an indictable offence, where once it never could, due to changes in the law to protect the female. Muggings and sexual attacks have become commonplace, and as the law does not allow a person to carry a weapon, is it any wonder women are turning to karate in their thousands?

Karate training will **not** make a woman muscle-bound, for being Arnold Schwarzenegger's female counterpart is not most women's idea of a body beautiful (nor is it most men's, come to that). On the contrary, it will tone the muscles, firm the body and generally make her more feminine and appealing.

Add to that a pastime that is inexpensive – one that can be practised alone and gives a marvellous outlet for frustration, and aggression – together with the chance to meet some very nice like-minded people, then the argument **for** women in karate is overwhelming.

1

ATTACKER GRABS BOTH WRISTS.

B

IF HE IS STRONG, FIRST KICK TO THE G▮

E

STEP FORWARD AND WITH BOTH HANDS PUSH ATTACKER AWAY.

A

2

ALTERNATIVE COUNTER ATTACK N▮ GRAB THE ATTACKER'S RIGHT WRIST ▮ THE LEFT HAND.

B

STEP IN STRIKING THE NECK WITH A KNIFE HAND STRIKE.

A

4

OPPONENT GRABS THE RIGHT WRIS▮

292

ST PALMS UPWARDS TO BREAK GRIP.

AS GRIP IS RELEASED PREPARE TO PUSH.

P IN AND ATTACK TO THE CHIN WITH A
M HEEL STRIKE. DO NOT LET GO OF THE
RIGHT WRIST.

3

ALTERNATIVE COUNTER ATTACK NO.2
HOLDING THE WRIST, BRING THE RIGHT
HAND TO THE LEFT EAR.

KE A FIST WITH THE RIGHT HAND AND
TAKE HOLD OF IT WITH THE LEFT.
START THE ATTACK BY TWISTING...

THE ATTACKER'S ARM IN ON HIMSELF AND
FINISH WITH A RISING ELBOW STRIKE TO THE
CHIN.

293

5

ATTACKER GRABS RIGHT WRIST.

PULL BACK AND BREAK THE GRIP.

ALTERNATIVE STRIKE NO.1 IS A BACKFIST TO THE RIBCAGE. HERE THE ARM SWINGS LATERALLY.

6

ALTERNATIVE STRIKE NO.2 IS AN UPWAR BACKFIST STRIKE TO THE GROIN.

8

ATTACKER COMES FROM BEHIND

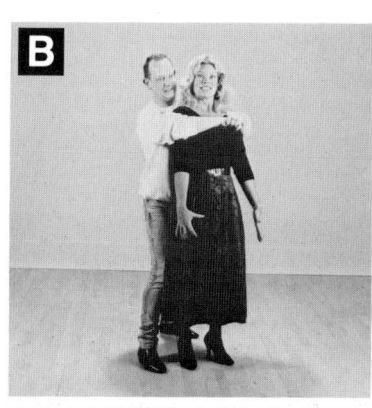

WITH A BEAR HUG OVER THE CHEST.

CONTINUE MOVING THE RIGHT ARM IN A CIRCULAR MOTION.

STEP IN AND STRIKE TO THE BRIDGE OF THE NOSE WITH A BACKFIST STRIKE.

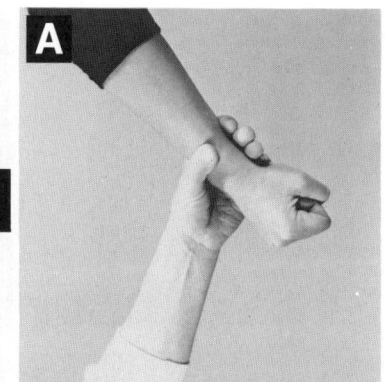

CLOSE-UP VIEW SHOWING THE GRAB...

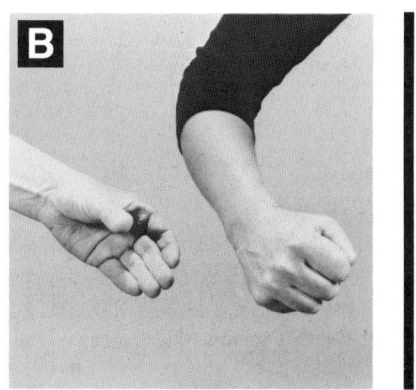

AND THE BREAK BETWEEN THE THUMB AND FINGERS.

DROP THE BODY LOW, SIMULTANEOUSLY RAISING BOTH ELBOWS TO BREAK THE GRIP.

COUNTER ATTACK TO THE SOLAR PLEXUS WITH A REVERSE ELBOW STRIKE, AUGMENTED WITH THE LEFT HAND.

295

9

ATTACKER PREPARES TO ATTACK FROM BEHIND.

USING A BEAR HUG LOW DOWN, HE TRA
THE UPPER ARMS.

10

IN A QUITE UNFORGIVABLE ACTION, THE ATTACKER MAKES HIS MOVE.

MAINTAINING HER DISTANCE, SHE SWII
BOTH ARMS BACKWARDS...

11

PICKING UP HER HIGH HEEL SHOE TO PROTECT HERSELF FROM THIS MUCH STRONGER MAN...

SHE STRIKES WITH HER FINGERS TO TI
EYES.

STILL ABLE TO MOVE HER LOWER RIGHT ARM SHE TWISTS HER BODY TO THE LEFT,

STRIKING THE UNPROTECTED GROIN WITH A KNIFEHAND STRIKE.

ND THEN FORWARDS, STRIKING BOTH S SIMULTANEOUSLY ABOVE THE ELBOW JOINTS.

BOTH ARMS ARE BROKEN BY THE FORCE OF THE PALM HEEL STRIKES.

USING THE HEEL AS A WEAPON

SHE DRIVES IT INTO THE MAN'S EYE: NORMALLY, NO ONE WOULD DREAM OF EVER DOING THIS. BUT IN A LIFE AND DEATH SITUATION, MANY WOULD.

297

HERE BASIC BLOCKS ARE USED TO GREAT ADVANTAGE. SOTO UDE UKE, AGE UKE, GEDAN BARAI AND KAKEWAKI UKE.

12

THE VICTIM IS GRABBED BY THE LEFT LAPEL.

USING THE TWISTING ACTION OF THE HIPS STEPPING BACK – SHE ATTACKS ABOVE THE ELBOW JOINT WITH SOTO UDE UKE.

15

THE ATTACKER GRABS THE RIGHT LAPEL.

STEPPING IN...

16

FROM THE FRONT, BOTH LAPELS ARE HELD.

USING A WEDGE BLOCK, PRISE BOTH ARMS APART. IF THE ATTACKER IS TOO STRONG FRONT GROIN KICK WOULD NOT GO AMISS.

298

THE ABOVE PHOTOGRAPH SHOWS THE SAME ATTACK BEING THWARTED BY AN AGE UKE.

THE MOMENT AN UPPER RISING BLOCK ON THE OTHER SIDE BECOMES AN ATTACK.

A RIGHT DOWNWARD BLOCK IS DELIVERED TO THE CROOK OF THE ARM, CAUSING THE ATTACKER TO INCLINE FORWARD.

THIS BRINGS HIS NECK INTO THE PERFECT POSITION FOR A DOWNWARD ELBOW STRIKE. (OTOSHI EMPI)

STEPPING THROUGH...

SWING THE RIGHT ARM IN A BIG ARC AND STRIKE THE GROIN WITH A RIDGE HAND STRIKE. (HAITO UCHI)

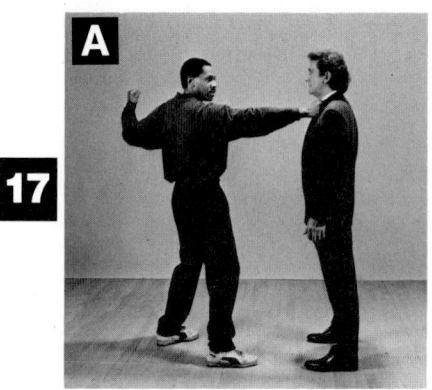

17

THE AGGRESSOR TAKES HOLD OF THE LEFT
LAPEL.

TAKE HOLD OF HIS RIGHT THUMB AN[
ATTACK TO THE EYES.

KEEP HOLD OF THE RIGHT HAND AS A WRIST
LOCK CAN BE APPLIED. KICK WITH THE
RIGHT LEG TO THE RIBS.

18

THE ATTACKER GRABS BOTH LAPEL[

DISTRACT HIM BY FIRST ATTACKING TO THE
EYES WITH THE RIGHT AND THEN LEFT.

SWEEP HIS RIGHT ARM ACROSS AND D[
APPLYING AN ARM LOCK.

THE RIGHT HAND UP FOR ADDITIONAL SUPPORT AND TWIST OUTWARDS.

SIMULTANEOUSLY STEP BEHIND WITH THE LEFT FOOT, USE THE HIPS AND THROW.

HE IS VERY STRONG MAKE A SLIGHT ADJUSTMENT TO THE POSITION OF HIS TESTICLES

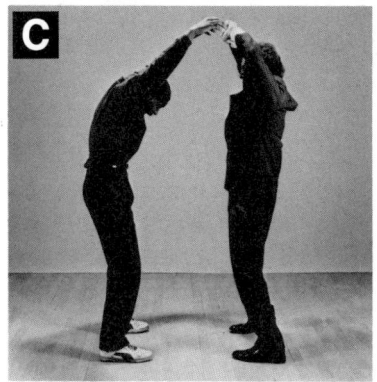

SWING BOTH ARMS UP AS IF PERFORMING TWO AGE UKES TOGETHER.

WITH THE LEFT HAND GRAB HIS HAIR

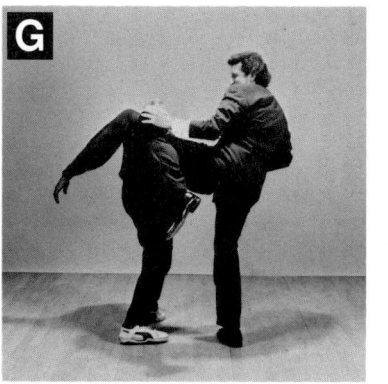

AND PULL HIS HEAD RIGHT BACK, SIMULTANEOUSLY BRINGING THE LEFT KNEE UP TO ATTACK HIS NECK.

IF THE HAIR IS PULLED FROM THE FRONT

BRING BOTH HANDS ON TOP OF THE ATTACKER'S HAND AND PULL DOWN TO RELIEVE THE PAIN.

BRING THE RIGHT HAND OVER AND TAKE HOLD OF THE LITTLE FINGER SIDE OF HIS HAND.

BRING THE LEFT HAND ON TO THE ATTACKER'S ARM FOR SUPPORT AND, AS THAT PROMINENT INSTRUCTOR MICK NURSE WAS HEARD TO SAY,"LOOSEN HIM UP".

IF THE RIGHT WRIST SHOULD BE GRABBED

EXPAND THE FINGERS OF THE RIGHT HAND THIS INCREASES THE WRIST GIRTH, SO LESSENING THE ATTACKER'S GRIP.

USING THE BACK LEG, SWING IT FORWARD
AND UP INTO HIS GROIN.

IF THE LEFT LAPEL SHOULD BE GRIPPED

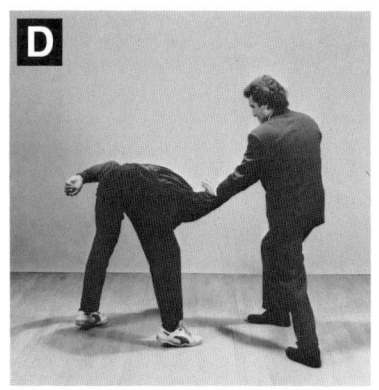

WITH BOTH HANDS, SWING THE RIGHT ARM
INTO AN ARMLOCK (BY SLIDING THE LEFT
HAND ABOVE THE ELBOW JOINT).

FINALLY, KICK TO THE FACE WITH THE RIGHT
INSTEP.

TWIST THE OPEN RIGHT HAND UPWARDS, SO
PUTTING PRESSURE ON HIS WRIST.

MOVE IN AND APPLY AN AUGMENTED
UPPER RISING ELBOW STRIKE TO THE CHIN.

22

THE ASSAILANT GRABS THE HAIR.

BRING THE LEFT HAND ON TOP OF HIS GRABBING HAND TO RELIEVE THE PRESSURE. BEGIN TO STEP IN.

BY PULLING SHARPLY TOWARDS YOU, THE ATTACKER WILL BE THROWN BACKWARDS AND BECOME AIRBORNE. (THIS IS NOT THE TIME TO ENQUIRE WHETHER OR NOT HE HAS A PILOT'S LICENCE).

INSTEAD...

23

THE ATTACKER LAUNCHES A RUGBY-STYLE TACKLE AT YOUR WAIST.

SLIDE THE RIGHT ARM UNDER HIS LEFT A THE LEFT HAND BEHIND HIS HEAD.

C

P IN AND DROP DOWN, PUNCHING TO
THE GROIN.

D

BEFORE HE CAN RECOVER, QUICKLY CLASP
BOTH HANDS BEHIND HIS KNEES.

G

LOW SUIT YOURSELF BY LEAPING INTO
THE AIR AND...

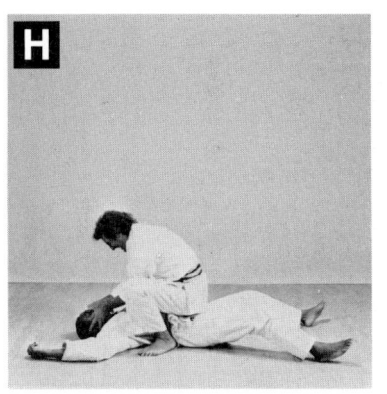

H

LANDING ON HIS CHEST, BRING YOUR
THUMBS INTO HIS EYES.

C

PPING BACK – CONTINUE HIS FORWARD
MENTUM BY TWISTING AND THROWING.

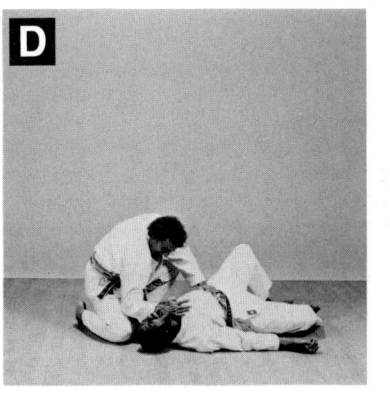

D

STRIKE WITH A KNIFE HAND STRIKE TO THE
THROAT OR NECK.

A

THE ATTACKER GRABS THE LEFT SHOULDER
FROM THE SIDE.

B

CATCH UNDER HIS RIGHT ARM AND
COUNTER ATTACK TO THE EYES.

E

CONTINUE SWEEPING AND PULLING.

F

AUTOMATICALLY, THE RIGHT HAND WILL
COME ON TOP READY FOR THE FINISHING
MOVE.

B

STEP THROUGH AND TO HIS RIGHT, TWIST
THE ARM (BACK OF FIST DOWN), EXECUTING
AN ARM LEVER USING YOUR SHOULDER AS
A FULCRUM.

C

AFTER BREAKING THE ARM – STRIKE WITH
LEFT REVERSE ROUNDHOUSE ELBOW STRIKE

DROP DOWN ON TO ONE KNEE AND PUNCH TO THE GROIN.

BRING THE RIGHT ARM DOWN IN A SCOOPING ACTION, AS CONTACT WITH THE LEG IS MADE, PULL DOWN WITH THE LEFT HAND.

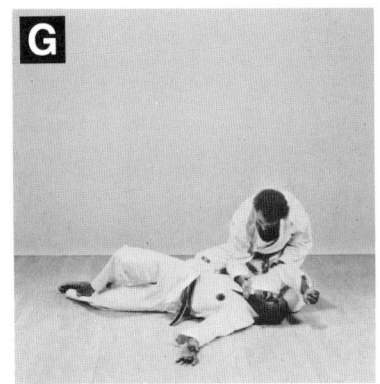

STRIKE IMMEDIATELY WITH A KNIFE HAND STRIKE TO THE NECK OR THROAT.

25

BLOCK AN UPPER PUNCH WITH AN X BLOCK AS THE RIGHT LEG MOVES BACK.

PIVOT ON THE LEFT FOOT AND SWEEP HIS FRONT LEG WITH YOUR RIGHT LEG.

QUICKLY COUNTER ATTACK USING THE FOOT EDGE TO THE RIB CAGE.

A

BLOCK AN UPPER PUNCH USING AN
X BLOCK.

B

TWIST THE ARM TO THE RIGHT AND DOWN
IN A CIRCULAR MOTION.

E

KEEP HOLD WITH YOUR LEFT HAND AND
SWING YOUR RIGHT ARM OVER HIS CHEST
AND BEHIND HIS HEAD.

F

AT THIS POINT HE IS COMPLETELY
POWERLESS. QUICKLY WITHDRAW THE L
HAND AND...

B

TURN IN AND STRIKE TO THE EYES.

C

RELEASE HIS GRIP BY EXECUTING A LE
UPPER RISING BLOCK.

C

P THROUGH TO THE OUTSIDE UNDER THE
RM YOU ARE HOLDING. TURN TO YOUR
EFT AND BRING HIS ARM UP HIS BACK.

D

AS HE TRIES TO ATTACK WITH HIS ONLY
FREE ARM DUCK UNDER HIS BACK FIST
STRIKE...

G

RIKE WITH A BOTTOM FIST STRIKE TO THE
GROIN.

27

A

BEING GRABBED FROM THE SIDE.

D

ATCH HIS RIGHT ARM WITH YOUR LEFT
D BRING YOUR RIGHT HAND BEHIND HIS
NECK.

E

PULL HIS HEAD FORWARD, BRINGING HIS
FACE IN CONTACT WITH YOUR RIGHT KNEE.

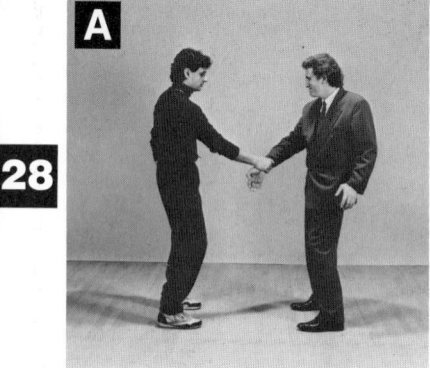

A

28

IN GOOD FAITH, YOU OFFER YOUR HAND TO SHAKE HANDS. INSTEAD – YOUR WRIST IS GRABBED.

B

PLACE YOUR LEFT HAND ON THE BACK OF HIS.

A

29

IN THE BEAR HUG FROM BEHIND, THE ARMS REMAIN FREE.

B

PRISE YOUR RIGHT HAND UNDER HIS LITTLE FINGER.

A

30

A BEAR HUG THAT LEAVES THE ARMS UNENCUMBERED.

B

LOOK AT THE BACK OF THE UPPERMOST HAND AND RAISE THE RIGHT FIST.

310

WIST YOUR RIGHT HAND IN A CLOCKWISE
RCULAR MOTION KEEPING THE LEFT HAND
IN PLACE.

TAKE HOLD OF HIS RIGHT WRIST AND ROLL
IT TOWARDS HIM. THIS ROLLING ACTION
HAS AN AMAZING EFFECT ON THE KNEES
AND CAUSES THEM TO BUCKLE.

HOLDING IT TIGHTLY, RIP IT BACKWARDS
ACROSS YOUR BODY.

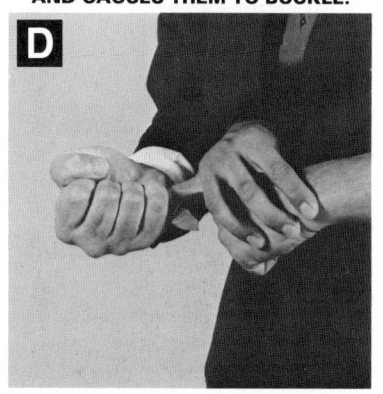

CLOSE-UP SHOT OF THE LITTLE FINGER JUST
PRIOR TO DISLOCATION.

TRIKE INTO THE CENTRE OF THE BACK OF
THE HAND WITH A ONE-KNUCKLE FIST.
REPEAT IF NECESSARY.

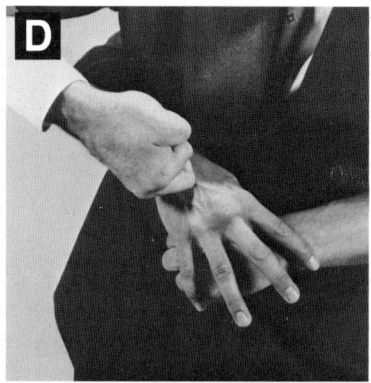

CLOSE-UP OF A ONE-KNUCKLE FIST
"MASSAGING" A VITAL SPOT.

Have you ever shaken hands with, (fortunately they are in a minority group) men who proceed to crush your hand in an effort to convince you they are very strong. What is more galling, is that their bone crushing antics are usual accompanied by a beaming smile. Uncannily, that smile remains intact for the whole duration of the greeting, causing our complex ridden chum to take on the guise of an amateur ventriloquist. The following defences will "Wipe the smile off his face".

31

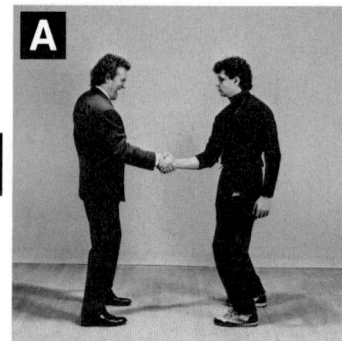

THE JAPANESE "BOW" WESTERNERS "SHAKE HANDS"

TWIST HIS HAND TURNING THE RIGHT PALM UPWARDS. STEP IN BRINGING THE LEFT ARM OVER HIS RIGHT.

YOUR LEFT ARM IS NOW BEAUTIFULLY POSITIONED FOR AN ELBOW STRIKE.
(BUT REMEMBER, YOU MAY WISH TO DO BUSINESS WITH THIS CHAP AND CONDUCTING IT FROM A HOSPITAL BED, MAY NOT ENHANCE YOUR CHANCES OF SUCCESS).

32

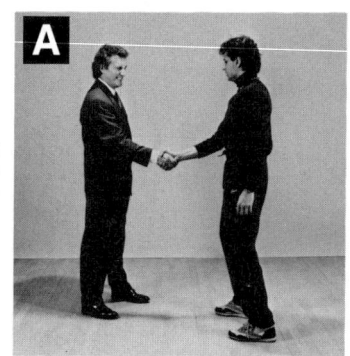

THE HANDSHAKE.

KEEPING HOLD OF HIS RIGHT HAND SWING YOUR RIGHT LEG UP READY FOR A HEEL KICK.

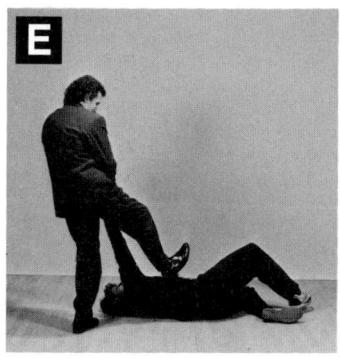

STRIKE HIS RIB CAGE WITH THE HEEL OF YOUR SHOE.

312

iously, meeting someone for the first time, despite their little problem does not give you the right to change his ysical appearance. The following defences taken "Just so far" will serve to remind him you have more up your eve than your arm.

C

ARRY ON DOWN IN A CIRCULAR ACTION.

D

SUPPORT HIS ARM UNDERNEATH BUT ABOVE THE ELBOW JOINT. PUSH DOWN WITH YOUR RIGHT HAND TO BREAK HIS ARM.

B

EAVE YOUR HAND IN HIS AND BEGIN TO URN TO YOUR LEFT A COMPLETE CIRCLE, INGING YOUR LEFT HAND ON TO HIS RIGHT.

C

WITH HIS LOSS OF BALANCE TWIST BOTH HANDS OUTWARDS.

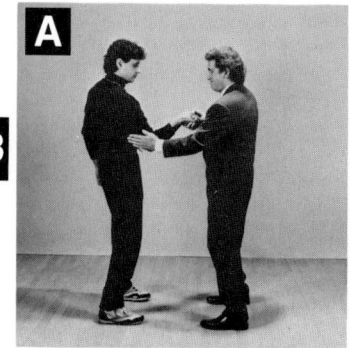

A

ACE THE LEFT HAND ON THE OUTSIDE OF HIS RIGHT ELBOW.

B

PUSH IN WITH THE LEFT HAND WHILE TWISTING OUT AND APPLYING A WRIST LOCK WITH THE RIGHT.

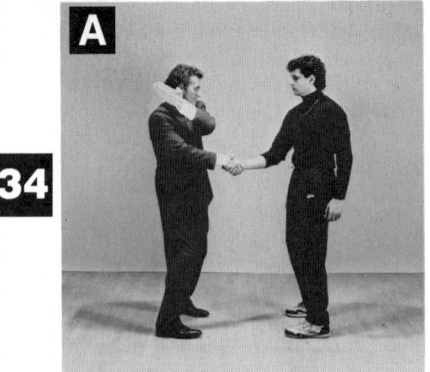

34

"THE PENNY HAS DROPPED" THIS IS NO
ORDINARY HAND-SHAKE SO FIRSTLY RAISE
THE LEFT HAND TO THE RIGHT EAR.

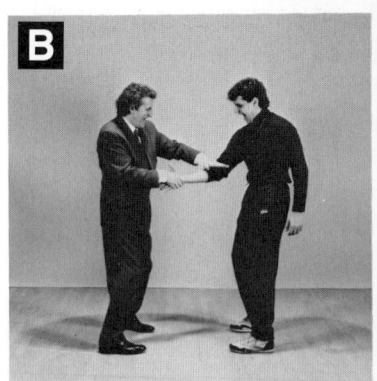

A SUCCESSFUL DISENGAGEMENT HERE
DEPENDS ON TIMING. THE KNIFE HAND STR
TO THE CROOK OF THE ARM MUST COINCI
WITH THE WITHDRAWAL OF THE RIGHT HA

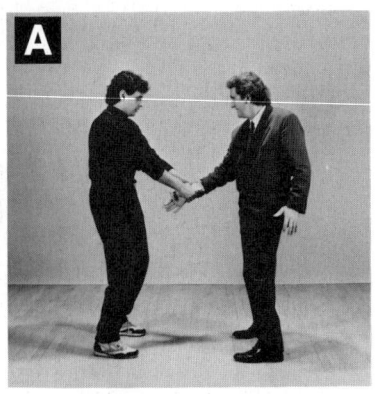

35

THE OPPONENT GRABS YOUR RIGHT WRIST
WITH TWO HANDS.

MOVE IN A LITTLE, MAKE A FIST WITH YC
RIGHT HAND, PASS YOUR LEFT ARM
BETWEEN HIS ARMS AND HOLD YOUR FI

36

THE ATTACKER GRABS THE RIGHT WRIST

USE THE STRONG MUSCLES ON THE RIG
HAND SIDE OF THE BODY TO HELP
WITHDRAW THE HAND TO THE WAIST

314

POWER SHOULD BE DIVIDED EQUALLY. 50% TO THE STRIKING HAND AND 50% TO THE WITHDRAWING ONE.

YOU ARE NOW IN A PERFECT POSITION TO DELIVER A STRAIGHT PUNCH – SHOULD IT BE NECESSARY.

TURN HIS HANDS BACK ON HIMSELF BY MOVING THE RIGHT ARM UP.

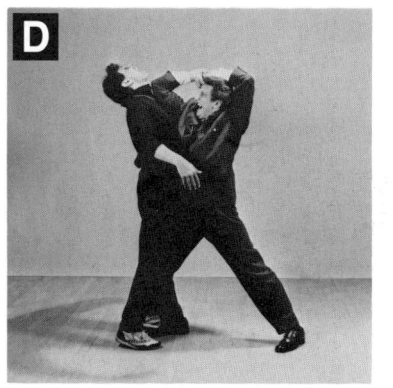

STEP RIGHT IN AND COMPLETE AN AUGMENTED UPPER RISING ELBOW STRIKE TO THE CHIN.

LOCK THE RIGHT HAND AT THE WAIST AND PIVOTING, TWIST THE HIPS SO THE STANCE FACES OUTWARDS. THE HAND IS EASILY RELEASED.

TWIST THE HIPS BACK BUT THIS TIME LET A BACK FIST STRIKE ACCOMPANY THEM.

ATTACKER COMES FROM THE REAR

AND PERFORMS A BEAR HUG VERY LOW DOWN TRAPPING HER ARMS COMPLETELY

SNAPPING HER LOWER RIGHT LEG UPWARDS, HER STILLETTO HEEL SCORES A DIRECT HIT ON ONE OF TWO TARGETS.

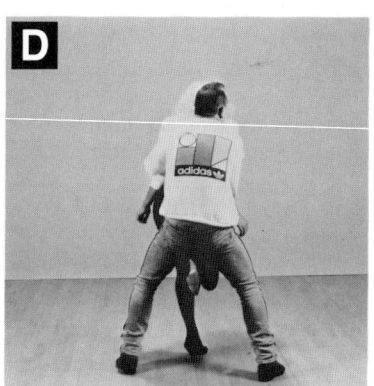

THIS IS THE PHOTOGRAPH THAT, WHEN TAKEN, BROUGHT TEARS TO THE CAMERAMAN'S EYES.

HOW TO CHOOSE A CLUB

Finding the right club for you can be a very hit or miss affair. It is possible to "make a go of it" with almost any club, instructor or style, but a little homework initially reduces the chances of you "dropping out" in the early stages by joining a club with maximum appeal and suitable to your personality and character. I suggest you follow a simple process of elimination.

1. Decide geographically where you would like to train and how far you are prepared to travel.
2. Contact the Martial Arts Commission in London telephone 081-691 3433 and ask them for the names and addresses of reputable instructors and clubs in your chosen area.
3. Compile a list of local clubs by visiting sports centres and collecting newspaper advertisements.
4. Talk to friends or personal contacts who already belong to a club. They naturally will have a strong bias in favour of their own club, so take this on board. Now, armed with a list of recommended clubs and their training times, visit them personally.

If your preference is for **sport karate,** look at the instructor, his experience as a competitor, ability to teach and communicate his competition skills, the success of the club in tournaments both locally and nationally. Finally, if many of the students are "bandaged to the hilt", it's a pretty good indication that injuries occur quite regularly and before long you would become just another statistic. Having said that, if you still find yourself driven by some masochistic urge to join, firstly check to see that your life assurance premiums are paid up to date!

On the other hand, your preference may be for **traditional karate.** If so, the teacher should set a good example to his students through discipline, etiquette, control and humility. He should have the ability to communicate to the class and consider the needs and requirements of the student on an individual basis. The underlying philosophy of karate-dō should run through the lesson and the analogy made between modern day living and ancient thinking. Whatever type of karate you wish to follow, that old adage, "you can fool some of the people some of the time . . . . . . " would seem to apply. Generally, if a teacher is good, he will attract a lot of good people – so a fair indicator is the size of a club and the numbers training.

Time spent looking at various clubs and talking to people is never wasted and before you realise it, the pieces of the jigsaw will have slotted into place and your club will be chosen for you.

THE RELATIONSHIP BETWEEN TEACHER AND STUDENT

In principle, the relationship between teacher and student is the same in the West as it is in the East. The reality differs considerably, and many Japanese students could be forgiven for thinking that Westerners have an attitude problem. Of course they don't, for the Western teacher is viewed by student and layman alike with *different eyes.*

The word for teacher in Japanese is *sensei*, and it's a little difficult to impart the feeling of respect and admiration that Japanese have for one who has been bestowed with this title.
This short story should demonstrate the point.

In the late 'sixties I accompanied Kanazawa sensei to a rendezvous in London with an old Japanese gentleman. I had not seen or heard of this man before, so you can imagine my surprise when, on meeting him, Kanazawa sensei, who was then 6th dan, bowed very low indeed and addressed the man as *"sensei"*. Throughout the long conversation he used the word "sensei" almost constantly and with great reverence. Sitting back in silence, I wondered what grade this master must be, and indeed, what art did he practise? He probably did them all!

On the way home, I just couldn't contain myself any longer. "Sensei," I said, "what grade is that old gentleman?" "No grade," replied Kanazawa sensei. "Then, what martial art does he practise?" "No martial art" came the answer. I paused for a moment. "Then why do you call him 'sensei'?" "Because he is a teacher – **a teacher of life**."

In time, I would come to understand the meaning of that remark – but not then.

Today, the word "sensei" is used for anyone who stands in front of a class. Students grading to black belt, in some cases, almost expect to be called "sensei".

A student of karate should be polite, respectful and courteous towards his sensei. He should have his teacher's welfare at heart and be prepared to protect his honour in both his presence and absence alike.

Most of all – he should be loyal.

BASIC RULES OF ETIQUETTE

Theoretically, the etiquette of karate-dō should not differ regardless of style, dojō, association or country – *but of course it does.* Bearing that in mind, a few simple rules will stand the beginner in good stead and should not cause any offence to his own instructor, and that is *very important.*

As basically a military art, karate puts great store in its ranking system. All belts are *earned*, not given away or bought, so the appropriate respect should be shown at all times.

1. Always be **punctual.**
2. Make sure your practice suit (Gi) is **clean** and folded correctly.
3. Smoking, eating or drinking is **not** permitted in the dojo.
4. **Toe** and **finger** nails should be cut regularly so as to prevent injury to other members.
5. **All** jewellery and personal adornments should be removed prior to training.
6. Do not **arrive** at the dojo in your "Karate Gi". Change into it when you get there.
7. Always bow to instructors and fellow students when seeing them for the **first time** and when departing.
8. Always remember the onus is on the **lower grade** to bow first.
9. Bow upon **entering** and **leaving** the dojo.
10. Bow before **joining** or **leaving** a class.
11. Bow after an instructor has **explained** something or **corrected** you.
12. In Japan, a student will enter a dojo and bow to all the instructors individually in order of **grade seniority**.
13. Always be polite and courteous to other karate-ka and extend this to **outside** the dojo.
14. On meeting a fellow karate-ka outside the dojo, a small low key but **correct bow** would not be out of place.
15. Endeavour to learn the "dojo kun" and incorporate it into your **daily life.**

The word "Oss" often accompanies a bow but in general, is only said to **people**. It is not usually said to inanimate objects.

One could quite easily fill a whole book when dealing with such a complex subject as Japanese protocol and etiquette. No one should reprimand you *severely* if your attitude is correct but you make a mistake out of ignorance. The Japanese are extremely polite people, but then again, they have had a lot of practice.

Just remember, **"manners are consideration for others"**, *and you will not go far wrong.*

THE CASE FOR CHILDREN IN KARATE

Even to the staunch traditionalist, karate training is forever changing and this is perfectly natural as our knowledge of the human body increases.

To the karate teacher, children are not miniature adults. Their physiology differs enormously as too do their levels and types of fitness. Childrens' bones are not fully formed and adult exercises can cause permanent damage. Bearing these points in mind, the case for childrens' involvement in karate cannot be ignored. Twenty years ago, the average karate class consisted of about 2% children and 98% adults. Today, 60% to 70% of students are children under the age of 14. The reason for this massive increase stems largely from, "just how beneficial karate training can be for young people". Most traditional martial arts have the same effect but I speak as a karate teacher only and one who has a very limited knowledge of other disciplines.

Children are taught from the outset that karate is primarily defensive and not offensive. They are taught never to use their fighting skills outside the training hall (dōjō), except in cases of extreme provocation and then only to defend. Apart from the physical aspects, everything else practised in the dōjō must be practised in the course of their life. For example:

Etiquette: A boy or girl during the first few weeks of their training learns and practises basic etiquette. They learn to be polite and respect their fellow students, instructor and parents. Soon, they become aware that good manners consist of having consideration for other people.

Discipline: Young people react to discipline very well considering how little they seem to get of it on the domestic front. Many parents often absolve themselves of all responsibility in this department, transferring the load to the already overburdened school teacher. Once a child has been disciplined for a short period, he then develops self-discipline and behaves correctly, of his own free will. His concentration is enhanced as he focuses his mind on the job in hand, whether it may be learning a sequence of complicated moves or passing an exam at school. Many parents notice a marked improvement in their childs' powers of concentration once karate training has commenced. Ironically however, very few are prepared to acknowledge publicly that the karate instructor may have been instrumental in achieving this.

In my opinion, children should not be made to think of themselves as failures. These "adults of tomorrow" should be encouraged in everything they do. How many times do you hear a parent shouting at a child, telling him "you're stupid" "you're terrible", "you should be ashamed of yourself". Say them enough and the child will think of himself and grow up, stupid, terrible and ashamed. On the other hand – praise, compliment and encourage him and you will have a child who is confident, well balanced and a pleasure to be with.

Self Confidence: Karate wins hands down on this score every time, but is it any wonder many children lack confidence in themselves? Just look at many parents – they do. From birth, children learn by mimicking the parents' actions. Can you blame a child for being tense and nervous after observing his parents desperate attempts to "make ends meet" and cope with the enormous pressures of 20th century living.

320

Traditional karate training helps prepare a child for life. I find it enormously encouraging when a mother or father who brings a child to lessons, does not just dump them, and head straight for the nearest pub, but instead, comes in the dōjō, sits down and takes an interest in what their child is learning. Children love to perform, especially to the people closest to them and they are far more clever than we give them credit for. How often are "little cries for help" disregarded. Rejection, to a child from questions like "come and play with me", or read, or walk or do anything, can be very hurtful, especially when the child has heard it one hundred times before. Answers like: "I haven't got time", "later", or "I'm busy", do nothing to inspire confidence.

When children come to my karate lessons, I tell them that for the next hour I'm going to treat them like adults. When the lesson is over, they will walk out of the dōjō and their parents and the world will treat them again like children. The response I get is nothing short of amazing. Just watching 7-year-olds standing next to grown men and women, learning together is quite something. The children know more is expected from them and with a little encouragement from the teacher, they rise to the occasion.

Fitness: As a method of keeping fit, karate is almost without equal. Many adults find it difficult to stay in good shape, whereas children find it a lot easier, consequently, they enjoy it more. A healthy body promotes a healthy mind.

Orderly and disciplined – Sensei knows the future of karate is safe in their hands.

A light hearted moment just prior to the grading examinations at Bedford recently.

Self-defence: Growing up in the early 'fifties, apart from scraps that all boys get into, I cannot remember seeing much street violence or hearing of muggings, although I'm sure it must have gone on. Forty years on, things do appear to have changed somewhat. Today, muggings take place in every town in the country. No longer are they the province of the elderly and now young people are considered "fair game". During the last five years we have witnessed the most bloody riots in Toxteth and Brixton with hundreds of innocent people and police officers being assaulted. Add to that "the peaceful protest" against the community charge that left Trafalgar Square looking more like Agincourt, and you have a reasonable case for learning self-defence.

Training for life: The psychological theme running through each lesson epitomises the triumph of good over evil. It encourages a gentlemanly code of conduct and the necessity to maintain standards. Discipline, etiquette and respect for one's elders all have their place in budo, the code of the military man. To relate, communicate and co-exist peaceably with one's fellow man is a worthy ideal worth striving for.

Success at school: Through constant repetition and self-analysis of physical techniques, relative perfection is ultimately acquired. Once this learning technique has become a habit, the principle will automatically be applied to most things by the sub-conscious. Indeed, many parents and school teachers have remarked how their child's powers of concentration have improved since starting karate training.Co-ordination obviously becomes much better as too does the child's awareness factor. The latter without doubt, plays a key role throughout a person's life.

THE DOJO KUN
MORALS OF THE DOJO

"Dojo Kun"

"Hitotsu! Jinkaku Kansei ni Tsutomuru Koto"
(One! To Strive For The Perfection of Character!)

"Hitotsu! Makoto No Michi O Mamoru Koto!"
(One! To Defend The Paths Of Truth!)

"Hitotsu! Doryoku No Seishin O Yashinau Koto!
(One! To Foster The Spirit Of Effort!)

"Hitotsu! Reigi O Omonzuru Koto!"
(One! To Honour The Principles of Etiquette!)

"Hitotsu! Kekki No Yu O Imashimuru Koto!"
(One! To Guard Against Impetuous Courage!)

The "Dojo Kun" is the Oath of the Karateka. Even today, it is recited at the end of each lesson at the Tokyo Headquarters of the Japan Karate Association, along with other Dojos in the J.K.A. Outside Japan I have not heard it, other than at training sessions of the Traditional Association of Shotokan Karate in Great Britain.

At the end of each lesson, the students and instructors line up to take the formal bow or "Rei", but before this and the usual "Mokuso" period, the whole class will sit in "Seiza" facing a shrine dedicated to Funakoshi Sensei.

The Dojo Captain or Senior Grade at the end of the two lines will shout out the "Dojo Kun", line at a time and immediately, the whole class will repeat each line back.

The Oath should always be chanted with strength, never mumbled in insincerity, for just as Karate movements should become automatic and reflexes conditioned, the simple Truths of the Oath should also penetrate the mind of the participant.

The "Dojo Kun" embodies all we are trying to achieve through the physical efforts of Karate training.

THE MATURE STUDENT

The mature student is a relatively new phenomenon and indeed a welcome one. For this, we have to thank changing attitudes amongst the top teachers of karate-dō during the last thirty years.

Once upon a time, karate, although looking very attractive to most age ranges, succeeded in *keeping* within its ranks only young men between the ages of seventeen and thirty with very few exceptions to the rule.

Karate needed to broaden its parameters to survive and grow. With the massive migration of karate-dō to the west, initiated primarily by the Japan Karate Association (J.K.A.) in the "sixties", the Japanese realised, that in giving westerners a little of what they wanted them to have, they also had to give the west a lot of what westerners wanted. Think about it.

It was all a question of balance and it took some time to get it right. By being too severe, the younger and older members of society were not attracted, or if they were, would quickly fall by the way-side. Apart from that, it was terribly counter productive to their aim, which was to spread the word. Eventually they did it – and most successfully too!

So what appeal does karate-dō have for the older person? Apparently – a great deal.

The mature student is capable of understanding the philosophy behind karate-dō and relating and applying it to his everyday life. His interest in fighting and tournaments is academic at the very best. So he finds the movements and application of kata delightful.

By exercising regularly, he improves his flexibility – already on the decline – becomes fitter and healthier and without doubt, looks and feels much younger.

The threat of arthritis with advancing years has receded, and breathing, the first thing he ever did and the last thing he will ever do, takes on a new significance. Add to that the possibility of research and the study of an art whose origins are lost in antiquity and you have an ideal student, who without doubt, will grace any dojō in the land.

The author expounding the virtues of karate-dō in 1987 to a well-known senior citizen. "I like the idea of a blue belt" she said "but exchanging it in 3 months time for a red one, well – I think I'd have to give that some serious consideration".

PREPARING FOR GRADING

"The first grading will be the worst, after that, you'll have nothing to worry about". That remark was made by a well-known instructor. I must confess, I never did agree with him, and nor would anyone with an iota of common sense.

Grading examinations are, in the main, **very traumatic occasions.** Children, on the whole, cope quite well, being used to frequent exams at school, whereas with many adults, it may be literally years since they sat any kind of examination. Older students tend to worry the most. On balance they take things more seriously, for they want to do a good job having **less time left** in which to do it. On grading day, a small percentage of people wonder what on earth they are doing there and begin to question their own sanity. Of course, to be blasé or over-confident prior to an exam, would be a mistake. You need to be keyed up and just a little anxious for the adrenalin to flow and so give your best.

Most karate associations nowadays conduct gradings four times a year, enabling students to exchange one coloured belt for another every twelve weeks, certainly up to 1st kyu. It is the responsibility of the instructor to prepare the student both physically and psychologically. No student should be put forward to grade if they have **no** chance of passing. A word of advice then to those attempting their first grades: your instructor will have taken you through the physical requirements of basics, kata and kumite. These should be practised at home as well as in the dōjō. If uncertainties arise, get him to deal with them early on or "as and when" they occur. It's a good idea to get a book that will compliment his teaching and he will advise you on the most suitable publication. In T.A.S.K. for example, students on a twelve week beginners course go through a process of learning new techniques and recapping on ones learnt in previous lessons. By the eleventh week, they go through a "mock" grading, performing the complete syllabus in class. Any problem areas are attended to and a noticeable air of confidence developed. In the last lesson before the examination, the i's are dotted and the t's crossed and the students know exactly what will be expected of them and perhaps more important – that they can do it.

Mention is made in a light-hearted way, *not* to go to any all-night parties the night before or have a six course lunch thirty minutes prior to the exam. The lesson concludes with some fun things, games or sumo wrestling etc, and they leave the dōjō in a conducive frame of mind. In conclusion, the grading examination brings the short-term benefit of a higher degree and an "obi" of a new and different colour. In the long-term, the rewards are less tangible but far more profound. Tests, obstacles, problems, challenges, call them what you will, the fact remains **– life is full of them.**

We all want to be successful and there is nothing wrong with that sentiment but perhaps to fail – just occasionally – is not such a bad thing. Remember, **"he who is always successful is not experienced in knowing how to deal with failure when it comes"**.

TASK GRADE ORDER BELT SYSTEM

Grade	Colour of Belt
Beginner	White Belt
10th Kyu	Blue Belt
9th Kyu	Red Belt
8th Kyu	Orange Belt
7th Kyu Intermediate	Orange with Yellow Stripe
7th Kyu	Yellow Belt
6th Kyu Intermediate	Yellow with Green Stripe
6th Kyu	Green Belt
5th Kyu Intermediate	Green with Purple Stripe
5th Kyu	Purple Belt
4th Kyu Intermediate	Purple with 1 White Stripe
4th Kyu	Purple with 2 White Stripes
3rd Kyu Intermediate	Purple with 1 Brown Stripe
3rd Kyu	Brown Belt
2nd Kyu Intermediate	Brown with 1 White Stripe
2nd Kyu	Brown with 2 White Stripes
1st Kyu Intermediate	Brown with 1 Red Stripe
1st Kyu	Brown with 2 Red Stripes
1st Dan Intermediate	Brown with 1 Black Stripe
1st Dan	Black Belt

The eight intermediate grades are for juniors under 14 years.

The intermediate grade syllabus is the same as for the next higher grade.

All grades given and ratified by T.A.S.K. are officially recognised by **The English Karate Governing Body** (E.K.G.B.) and the **World Union of Karate Organisations.**

T.A.S.K. Chief Instructor and Examiner: Sensei J. van Weenen, 6th Dan.

10th KYU – BLUE BELT

Basics

Technique	Stance	No	Comment
Choku-zuki	Shizentai	10	Facing forward
Gyaku-zuki	Zenkutsu	5	Left and right
Oi-zuki	Zenkutsu	5	Turn, same back
Age-uke	Zenkutsu	5	Turn, same back
Uchi-uke	Zenkutsu	5	Turn, same back
Gedan barai	Zenkutsu	5	Turn, same back
Mae-geri	Zenkutsu	5	Turn, same back

Kumite
Gohon kumite – 5 attack sparring (pages 206 and 207)
Upper level only to count

Kata
Taikyo-ku shodan
First half only, fast to count

N.B. Only English terminology will be used in this examination

9th KYU – RED BELT

Basics

Technique	Stance	No	Comment
Choku-zuki	Shizentai	10	Facing forward
Gyaku-zuki	Zenkutsu	5	Left and right
Oi-zuki	Zenkutsu	5	Turn, same back
Age-uke	Zenkutsu	5	Turn, same back
Soto-ude-uke	Zenkutsu	5	Turn, same back
Uchi-uke	Zenkutsu	5	Turn, same back
Mae-geri	Zenkutsu	5	Turn, same back
Yoko geri keage	Kiba	3	Turn, same back
Yoko geri kekomi	Kiba	3	Turn, same back

Kumite
Gohon kumite – Jōdan and Chūdan no count (pages 206–209)

Kata
Taikyo-ku Shodan
Fast no count

8th KYU – ORANGE BELT

Basics

Technique	Stance	No	Comment
Choku-zuki	Shizentai	10	Facing forward
Gyaku-zuki	Zenkutsu	5	Left and right
Oi-zuki	Zenkutsu	5	Forward and back
Age-uke	Zenkutsu	5	Forward and back
Soto-ude-uke	Zenkutsu	5	Forward and back
Uchi-uke	Zenkutsu	5	Forward and back
Shutō uke	Kōkutsu	5	Forward and back
Mae-geri	Zenkutsu	5	Turn, same back
Yoko geri keage	Kiba	3	Turn, same back
Yoko geri kekomi	Kiba	3	Turn, same back

Kumite
Kihon ippon kumite – Set 1 (page 262)
Attack Jōdan, Chūdan, Mae-geri from left stance followed by the same from right stance (one attack at each level)

Kata
Heian shodan, plus any previous kata

7th KYU – YELLOW BELT

Basics

Technique	Stance	No	Comment
Oi-zuki	Zenkutsu	5	Forward and back
Age-uke/Gyaku-zuki	Zenkutsu	5	Forward and back
Soto-ude-uke/ Gyaku-zuki	Zenkutsu	5	Forward and back
Uchi-uke/Gyaku-zuki	Zenkutsu	5	Forward and back
Shutō uke/Nukite	Kōkutsu	5	Forward and back
Mae-geri	Zenkutsu	5	Turn, same back
Yoko geri keage	Kiba	3	Turn, same back
Yoko geri kekomi	Kiba	3	Turn, same back

Kumite
Sanbon kumite, Attack Jōdan, Chūdan, Mae-geri (pages 219–223)
First perform attacks from left stance – then from right

Kata
Heian Nidan, plus any previous kata

6th KYU – GREEN BELT

Basics

Technique	No	Comment
Sanbon-zuki	5	Turn, same back
Age-uke/Gyaku-zuki/Gedan barai	5	Forward and back
Uchi-uke/Gyaku-zuki/Gedan barai	5	Forward and back
Shutō-uke/Mae-kizami-geri/Nukite	5	Forward and back
Ren-geri-jōdan-chūdan	3	Turn, Chūdan-jōdan
Yoko-geri-keage	3	Turn, same back
Yoko-geri-kekomi	3	Turn, same back
Mawashi-geri	5	Turn, same back

Kumite
Kihon ippon kumite – Set 2 (page 262)
Attack left Jōdan, Chūdan and Mae-geri, then repeat on the right

Kata
Heian sandan, plus any previous kata

5th KYU – PURPLE BELT

Basics

Technique	No	Comment
Sanbon-zuki	5	Forward and back
Age-uke/Mae-geri/Gyaku-zuki	5	Forward and back
Soto-ude-uke/Yoko Empi/Uraken	5	Forward and back
Uchi-uke/Kizami-zuki/Gyaku-zuki	5	Forward and back
Shutō-uke/Mae-kizami-geri/Nukite	5	Forward and back
Mae-geri/Oi-zuki	3	Turn, Mae-geri/Gyaku-zuki
Mae-ren-geri Chūdan, Jōdan	3	Turn, same Jōdan-chūdan
Ren-geri Mae-geri/Mawashi-geri	3	Turn, Mawashi-geri/Mae-geri
Ren-geri Mae-geri/Kekomi	3	Turn, Kekomi/Mae-geri

Kumite
Kihon ippon kumite – Set 3 (page 262)
Attack 5 different attacks with the left – then repeat on the right

Kata
Heian Yondan, plus any previous kata

4th KYU – PURPLE BELT WITH 2 WHITE STRIPES

Basics   **No**

1. Sanbon-zuki 5 times – *Turn* – Mae-geri/Sanbon-zuki   5

2. Age-uke/Mae-geri/Gyaku-zuki/Gedan-barai   5
    Stepping back the same

3. Soto-ude-uke/Yoko-empi/Uraken/Gyaku-zuki/Gedan-barai   5
    Stepping back the same

4. Uchi-uki (Kōkutsu dachi), Kizami-zuki/Gyaku-zuki/   5
    Gedan-barai (Zenkutsu dachi)
    Stepping back the same

5. Shūto-uke/Mae-kizami-geri/Nukite   5
    Stepping back the same

6. Mae-geri/Mawashi-geri/Uraken/Gyaku-zuki/Gedan-barai   3
    Turn – same back

7. Mae-geri/Kekomi/Shūto-uchi/Gyaku-zuki/Gedan-barai   3
    Turn – same back

8. Yoko-geri-keage (Kiba dachi), Gyaku-zuki (Zenkutsu dachi),
    Gedan-barai (Kiba dachi)   3
    Turn – same back

Kumite
Kihon ippon kumite – Set 4 (page 262)
Attack 5 different attacks with the left, then repeat on the right

Kata
Heian Godan, plus any previous kata

3rd KYU – BROWN BELT

Basics

		No
1.	Sanbon-zuki 5 times – *Turn* – Mae-geri/Sanbon-zuki	5
2.	Age-uke/Mae-geri/Gyaku-zuki/Gedan-barai *Stepping back the same*	5
3.	Soto-ude-uke/Yoko-empi/Uraken/Gyaku-zuki/Gedan-barai *Stepping back the same*	5
4.	Uchi-uki (Kōkutsu dachi), Kizami-zuki/Gyaku-zuki/ Gedan barai (Zenkutsu dachi) *Stepping back the same*	5
5.	Shutō-uke/Mae-kizami-geri/Nukite *Stepping back the same*	5
6.	Mae-geri/Mawashi-geri/Uraken/Gyaku-zuki/Gedan-barai *Turn – same back*	3
7.	Mae-geri/Kekomi/Shutō-uchi/Gyaku-zuki/Gedan-barai *Turn – same back*	3
8.	Yoko-geri-keage (Kiba dachi), Gyaku-zuki (Zenkutsu dachi), Gedan-barai (Kiba dachi) *Turn – same back*	3
9.	Ushiro geri from Zenkutsu dachi *Turn – same back*	3
10.	Face the front in Zenkutsu dachi Mae-geri to the front, kekomi to the side with same leg *Same with opposite leg*	3

Kumite

Kihon ippon kumite – Set 5 (page 262)
Attack 5 times with the left side, then repeat on the right

Jiyu-ippon-kumite – Set 1 (page 288)
Attack with right side only – Jōdan, chūdan and mae-geri

Kata

Tekki Shodan, plus any previous kata

2nd KYU – BROWN BELT WITH 2 WHITE STRIPES

Basics	No
1. Sanbon-zuki 5 times – *Turn* – Mae-geri/Sanbon-zuki	5
2. Age-uke/Mae-geri/Gyaku-zuki/Gedan-barai *Stepping back the same*	5
3. Soto-ude-uke/Yoko-empi/Uraken/Gyaku-zuki/Gedan-barai *Stepping back the same*	5
4. Uchi-uki (Kōkutsu dachi), Kizami-zuki/Gyaku-zuki/ Gedan-barai (Zenkutsu dachi) *Stepping back the same*	5
5. Shutō-uke/Mawashi-kizami-geri/Nukite *Stepping back the same*	5
6. Mae-geri/Mawashi-geri/Uraken/Gyaku-zuki/Gedan-barai *Turn – same back*	3
7. Mae-geri/Kekomi/Shutō-uchi/Gyaku-zuki/Gedan-barai *Turn – same back*	3
8. Yoko-geri-keage (Kiba dachi), Gyaku-zuki (Zenkutsu dachi), Gedan-barai (Kiba dachi) *Turn – same back*	3
9. Ushiro-geri/Gyaku-zuki *Turn – same back*	3
10. Face the front in Zenkutsu dachi. Mae-geri/Kekomi with the same leg. Mae-geri/Mawashi-geri with the same leg *Same with opposite leg*	3

Kumite

Kihon-ippon-kumite (page 262). Any set of the examiner's choice. Attacking from both sides

Jiyū-ipon-kumite – Set 2 (page 288). Attack with both sides, jōdan, chūdan and mae-geri

Kata

Bassai Dai, plus any previous kata

1st KYU – BROWN BELT WITH 2 RED STRIPES

Basics	No
1. Sanbon-zuki 5 times – *Turn* – Mae-geri/Sanbon-zuki	5
2. Age-uke/Mae-geri/Gyaku-zuki/Gedan-barai *Stepping back the same*	5
3. Soto-ude-uke/Yoko-empi/Uraken/Gyaku-zuki/Gedan-barai *Stepping back the same*	5
4. Uchi-uki (Kōkutsu dachi), Kizami-zuki/Gyaku-zuki/ Gedan-barai (Zenkutsu dachi) *Stepping back the same*	5
5. Shutō-uke/Mawashi-kizami-geri/Nukite *Stepping back the same*	5
6. Mae-geri/Mawashi-geri/Uraken/Gyaku-zuki/Gedan-barai *Turn – same back*	3
7. Mae-geri/Kekomi/Shutō-uchi/Gyaku-zuki/Gedan-barai *Turn – same back*	3
8. Yoko-geri-keage (Kiba dachi), Gyaku-zuki (Zenkutsu dachi), Gedan-barai (Kiba dachi) *Turn – same back*	3
9. Ushiro-geri/Gyaku-zuki *Turn – same back*	3
10. Kekomi (front leg), Mae-geri (back leg), step forward *Turn – same back*	3
11. Face the front in Zenkutsu dachi. Mae-geri/Kekomi with the same leg. Mae-geri/Mawashi-geri with the same leg. Mae-geri/Kekomi/Ushiro-geri with the same leg *Same with opposite leg*	3

Kumite
Kihon-ippon-kumite – Sets 1–5 (page 262). Right attack only

Jiyū-ipon-kumite – Set 3 (page 288). Left attacks first,
followed by right attacks

Kata
A choice of one of the following:
Kanku-dai, Enpi, Jion, Jitte, Ji'in, plus any previous kata

SHODAN – BLACK BELT. 1st DEGREE

All Kihon and combination techniques are performed from Jiyu dachi

Basics   **No**

1. Kizami-zuki/Mae-geri/Sanbon-zuki. *Turn same back*   3

2. Age-uke/Mae-geri/Gyaku-zuki/Gedan-barai   5
   Stepping back the same

3. Soto-ude-uke/Yoko-empi/Uraken/Gyaku-zuki/Gedan-barai   5
   Stepping back the same

4. Uchi-uke (Kōkutsu dachi), Kizami-zuki/Gyaku-zuki/   5
   Gedan-barai
   Stepping back the same

5. Shūto-uke/Mawashi-kizami-geri/Nukite   5
   Stepping back the same

6. Mae-geri/Mawashi-geri/Uraken/Gyaku-zuki/Gedan-barai   3
   Turn – same back

7. Mae-geri/Kekomi/Shutō-uchi/Gyaku-zuki/Gedan-barai   3
   Turn – same back

8. Gyaku-zuki/Mae-geri/Mawashi-geri/Turn/Shutō-uke/Gyaku-zuki   3
   Turn – same back

9. Step back, Age-uke, step forward Mawashi-geri (back leg),   3
   Uraken/Oi-zuki. *Turn same back*

10. Mawashi-kizami-geri/Ushiro-geri/Uraken/Gyaku-zuki   3
    Turn – same back

11. Kizami kekomi, step forward Mae-geri/Oi-zuki/Gyaku-zuki   3
    Turn – same back

12. Stepping in Kiba dachi, Keage/Kekomi with the same leg   3
    Turn – same back

13. Face the front in Zenkusu dachi. Mae-geri/Kekomi/Ushiro-geri   3
    Repeat on opposite side

Kumite
Kihon-ippon-kumite – Sets 1–5, attacking from both sides.
Jiyu-ippon-kumite – Sets 1–5, attacking from both sides.
Freestyle sparring (Jiyu kumite) against two consecutive dan grades.

Kata
A choice of one of the following:
Kanku-dai, Enpi, Jion, Jitte, Ji'in, Gankaku or Hangetsu
plus previous kata
Oral examination to assess student's character.

NIDAN – BLACK BELT. 2nd DEGREE

Basics

Basics are the same as for Shodan with the addition of:

Kizami kekomi/Ushiro geri/Shutō uchi/Gyaku zuki three times. Turn same back.

On the same leg, Mae geri/Kekomi/Ushiro geri/Mawashi geri and return to the starting position. Repeat on the other side.

Kumite

Jiyu ippon kumite. Sets 1–5, attack from both sides.

Okuri jiyu ippon kumite (two attacks), first specified, second free.

Specified attacks are: one Jōdan, one Chūdan, one Mae geri, one Kekomi, one Mawashi geri and one Ushiro geri.

Jiyu kumite against three consecutive dan grades of Nidan status.

Kata

Tokui kata with explanation of Bunkai.

Plus any previous kata.

Oral examination as in Shodan.

SANDAN – BLACK BELT. 3rd DEGREE

Basics

Demonstration of all basic Shotokan techniques against a stationary target.

Kumite

Jiyu kumite against five consecutive Sandans. Minimum non-stop fighting time: 10 minutes.

Kata

Tokui kata plus interpretation of Bunkai.

Any other previous kata of the examiner's choice.

Demonstration of teaching ability.

Oral examination as in Nidan.

1-100 ENGLISH - JAPANESE

1 – ICHI	35 – SANJYU GO	69 – ROKUJYU KU
2 – NI	36 – SANJYU ROKU	70 – SHICHIJYU
3 – SAN	37 – SANJYU SHICHI	71 – SHICHIJYU ICHI
4 – SHI	38 – SANJYU HACHI	72 – SHICHIJYU NI
5 – GO	39 – SANJYU KU	73 – SHICHIJYU SAN
6 – ROKU	40 – YONJYU	74 – SHICHIJYU SHI
7 – SHICHI	41 – YONJYU ICHI	75 – SHICHIJYU GO
8 – HACHI	42 – YONJYU NI	76 – SHICHIJYU ROKU
9 – KU	43 – YONJYU SAN	77 – SHICHIJYU SHICHI
10 – JYU	44 – YONJYU SHI	78 – SHICHIJYU HACHI
11 – JYU ICHI	45 – YONJYU GO	79 – SHICHIJYU KU
12 – JYU NI	46 – YONJYU ROKU	80 – HACHIJYU
13 – JYU SAN	47 – YONJYU SHICHI	81 – HACHIJYU ICHI
14 – JYU SHI	48 – YONJYU HACHI	82 – HACHIJYU NI
15 – JYU GO	49 – YONJYU KU	83 – HACHIJYU SAN
16 – JYU ROKU	50 – GOJYU	84 – HACHIJYU SHI
17 – JYU SHICHI	51 – GOJYU ICHI	85 – HACHIJYU GO
18 – JYU HACHI	52 – GOJYU NI	86 – HACHIJYU ROKU
19 – JYU KU	53 – GOJYU SAN	87 – HACHIJYU SHICHI
20 – NIJYU	54 – GOJYU SHI	88 – HACHIJYU HACHI
21 – NIJYU ICHI	55 – GOJYU GO	89 – HACHIJYU KU
22 – NIJYU NI	56 – GOJYU ROKU	90 – KYUJYU
23 – NIJYU SAN	57 – GOJYU SHICHI	91 – KYUJYU ICHI
24 – NIJYU SHI	58 – GOJYU HACHI	92 – KYUJYU NI
25 – NIJYU GO	59 – GOJYU KU	93 – KYUJYU SAN
26 – NIJYU ROKU	60 – ROKUJYU	94 – KYUJYU SHI
27 – NIJYU SHICHI	61 – ROKUJYU ICHI	95 – KYUJYU GO
28 – NIJYU HACHI	62 – ROKUJYU NI	96 – KYUJYU ROKU
29 – NIJYU KU	63 – ROKUJYU SAN	97 – KYUJYU SHICHI
30 – SANJYU	64 – ROKUJYU SHI	98 – KYUJYU HACHI
31 – SANJYU ICHI	65 – ROKUJYU GO	99 – KYUJYU KU
32 – SANJYU NI	66 – ROKUJYU ROKU	100 – HYAKU
33 – SANJYU SAN	67 – ROKUJYU SHICHI	
34 – SANJYU SHI	68 – ROKUJYU HACHI	

WEIGHT TRAINING FOR THE MARTIAL ARTIST

In the past it was thought, if a martial artist used weights to increase his strength, he would become **muscle-bound, slow and lethargic.** Nothing could be further from the truth, providing a few simple rules are observed. Testimony to this, particularly when thinking of Shotokan exponents is the K.U.G.B.'s **Terry O'Neill.** In recent years whilst getting older (he will probably deny it), he has also got **bigger, stronger** and to many people's dismay, paired up with him for Kihon or Jiyū Ippon Kumite – **faster.**

With correct training (weights) followed by **good stretching** (Karate stretching exercises are fine), the martial art can be improved, rather than impeded. Stretching helps to avoid stiffness and soreness and aids muscle recovery.

As a beginner, introduce your body to weight training gently, never lift heavy weights early on in your programme as this will only cause injury.

Before commencing, get a stress test by your G.P., and providing the results are favourable, take 6 – 8 weeks **"to get to know"** the weights, the movements and your capabilities. Find out about **nutrition,** as this is essential for building muscle and strength. A balanced diet of protein, carbohydrates, vitamins, fats and water is necessary to allow you to get the most from your training.

Almost all the strength built from weight training depends on the **intensity** of the workout. Keep the muscles working constantly during the exercise and aim for **high-intensity.** Make sure you are in control of the movement and take only short rests between sets.

The maximum benefit gained from a workout takes place between 20 to 40 minutes of the session, so the duration of the training session may be 45 minutes but never longer than one hour.

Keep strict form throughout all the exercises and concentrate (focus) your mind into the muscle you are working. Use **slow,** controlled movements as well as **fast explosive** ones, avoid bouncing or jerking and always utilise the full range of motion.

The exercises offered here are perfect for introducing weights into your fitness and Karate programme and as you progress, so the routine can be updated.

Training correctly with weights, coupled with the **appropriate stretching,** will not only improve your overall strength but will give you a great physique, improved confidence and a better understanding of the human body, without any detriment to speed whatsoever.

Finally, I would like to thank **Donovan Slue** for his patience in posing for so many fine photographs. Donovan has trained at the T.A.S.K. Hombu at **Bedford** for 20 years, is a **San Dan in Shotokan Karate** and is one of my most experienced instructors.

FLAT BENCH PRESS (No.1)

The Muscles:- Pectorals, Front Deltoids, Triceps.

The Movements:- Lie flat on the bench with feet on the floor, assume a medium grip on the bar, hands shoulder width apart. Lift the bar off and hold it over the chest at arms length. Lower the bar slowly to about 1" from the chest, keeping the elbows pointed outwards. The bar should come to a complete stop in the downwards position, (do not bounce it off your chest). Now press the bar up until your arms are locked. Always use a full range of motion. Breath in on the way down, and out on the way up.

 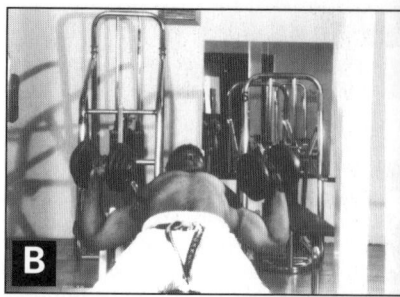

INCLINE DUMBELL PRESS (No.2)
The Muscles:- Upper Chest, Front Deltoids
The Movements:- Lie back on an incline bench (about 38° – 45°) dumbells in hand. Lift the dumbells and hold them straight above the head with the arms slightly bent. Now lower the weight down to the chest keeping the elbows pointing outwards. Stop, then press back up to the starting position. Breath in on the way down, and out on the way up.

FLAT FLYS (No.3)
The Muscle:- Pectorals
The Movement:- Lie flat on a bench holding dumbells at arms length above your head with your palms facing inwards. Now lower the weights out and down as far as you can, feeling the stretch across your chest, don't rotate your wrist or arm at any point in the lift. Bend the elbows slightly to reduce stress on joints. Be sure to flex the chest at the top. Breath in on the wide part, and out on the narrow part.

WIDE GRIP PULLDOWN (No.4)
The Muscles:- Latissimus Dorsi, Upper Back
The Movement:- Seated at the Pull Down machine and using a wide grip, pull the bar down behind your head until it touches your neck. Inhale as you bring the bar down, exhale as you release the bar to the starting position and be sure to squeeze the shoulder blades together when you bring the bar down.

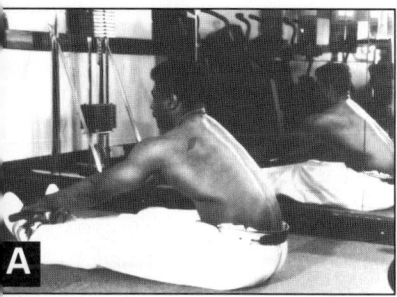 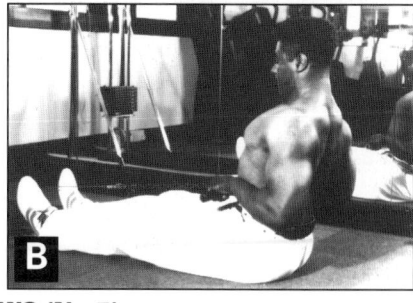

SEATED PULLEY ROWS (No.5)

The Muscles:- Latissimus Dorsi, Rhomboids, Erector Spinae

The Movements:- Using a floor level pulley, grasp the handle and lean forward with the legs slightly bent. Fully extend your arms to stretch right up both sides of the Lats. Now pull the handle back as far as possible into your waist. Keep the elbows bent and the chest high, and feel your back muscles contract. Breath out on the extended part of the exercise, in on the contracted part

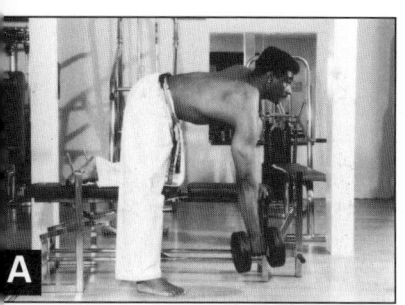 

ISOLATING DUMBELL ROW (No.6)

The Muscles:- Latissimus Dorsi, Rhomboids

The Movements:- Grasp a dumbell in one hand, and put the other hand and knee on a bench, position the leg on the side holding the dumbell firmly on the floor. Hold the dumbell at arms length and lift the weight up as high as you can into your waist. Contract the back muscles then lower the weight slowly feeling the stretch in your Lats. Repeat for the other side switching foot and hand positions accordingly. Do one complete side then the other.

BEHIND NECK PRESS (No.7)

The Muscles:- Front and Side Deltoids, also involves **Triceps**

The Movements:- This exercise can be done standing but being seated makes the movements stricter. Lift the bar off the rack and lower it behind the neck to just about an inch above the shoulders, then press the weight up to the starting position. Use a slightly wider than shoulder grip and keep the elbows as far back as possible.

LATERAL RAISES (No.8)

The Muscles:- Front Deltoids, Subscapularis, Teres Major, Latissimus Dorsi

The Movements:- Hold two dumbells together in front of you at arms length. Now slowly lift the weight up and out to either side, turning your wrist at the top as if pouring water, so that the rear of the dumbell is higher than the front. Finish movement at about ear level, then slowly lower the weight down to the starting position. Make sure you use your shoulders (do not swing the weight) and keep your arms straight.

REVERSE FLYS (No.9)

The Muscles:- **Rear** and **Middle Deltoids, Middle Trapezius, Rhomboids**

The Movements:- Standing up, bend from the waist keeping the back flat, holding the dumbells at arms length under you. Now raise the weight out to head level keeping your elbows slightly bent. Feel your deltoids contract by trying to touch your shoulder blades together behind you, then lower the weight slowly back to the starting position. Keep the dumbells aligned with the shoulders and the palms facing downwards.

SHRUGS (No.10)

The Muscles:- Upper Trapezius, Rhomboids

The Movements:- Stand erect with the arms at your side and a dumbell in each hand. Raise your shoulders as high as possible, as though you were trying to touch your ears with your shoulder blades. Hold, then return slowly to the starting position.

SQUATS (No.11)

The Muscles:- Quadriceps

The Movements:- Stand under a barbell that is positioned on a rack and let it rest across your shoulders. Hold on to the bar to balance it. Raise the bar off the rack and step into position, with your feet flat on the floor and keeping your head up and your back straight, bend your knees and lower yourself until your thighs are parallel to the floor. Now push yourself back up to the starting position (do not bounce). Your foot position determines which area of the thigh you'll be emphasising. A wide stance works the inner part of your thigh and a narrow stance stresses the outer part of the thigh.

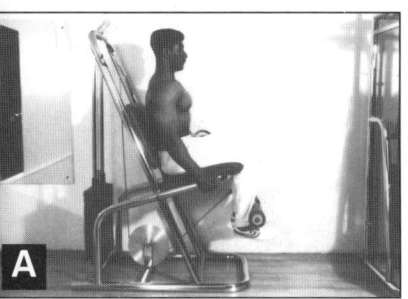 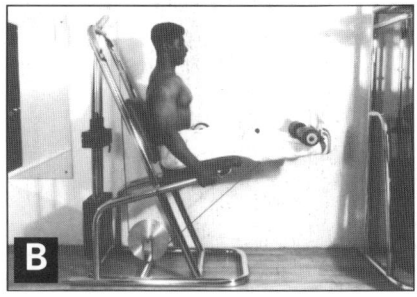

LEG EXTENSIONS (No.12)

The Muscles:- Quadriceps

The Movements:- Sit on the seat of a leg extension machine and hooking your feet under the pads, extend your legs out as far as possible. Flex your thighs and slowly lower the weight just short of the starting position, (do not drop the weight), and keep a continual pressure on your quadriceps.

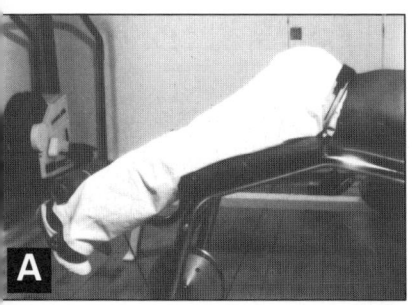 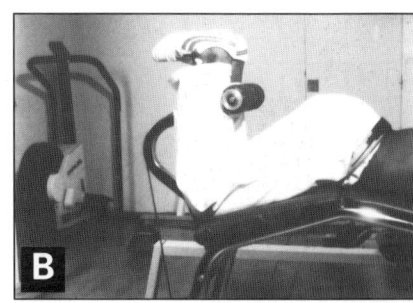

LEG CURL (No.13)

The Muscles:- Hamstrings

The Movements:- Lie facedown on the leg curl machine with your heels hooked under pads of the machine. Your legs should be straight in the starting position and keeping your body flat on the bench, curl the legs up as far as possible. Feel the contraction in your hamstrings, then slowly lower the weight back to the starting position. Always use a full range of motion in this exercise.

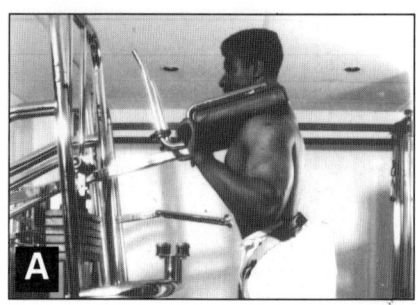 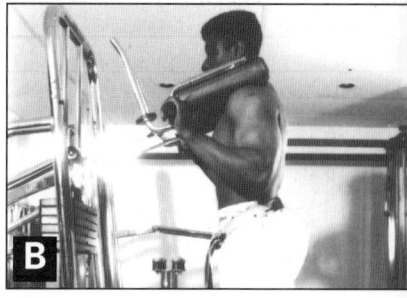

STANDING CALF RAISES (No.14)

The Muscles:- Gastrocnemius, Soleus

The Movements:- Stand with the ball of your foot on the block of a Standing Calf Raising Machine, your heels extended out in space. Slide your shoulders under the pads, and straighten your legs – this should lift the weight clear of the support. Now lower your heels as far as possible towards the floor, keeping your legs straight throughout the movement. Feel your calf muscles stretch fully at the bottom of the movement, then raise up on to your toes as high as possible. Contract the muscles then start again until desired repetitions have been achieved.

BICEPS (BARBELL) CURL (No.15)

The Muscles:- Biceps, Brachialis, Brachioraous

The Movements:- This exercise can be performed using dumbells or a barbell whilst standing, or seated using dumbells only. Using an underhand grip, your hands should be about shoulder width apart. Let the bar hang down in front of you, curl the bar out and up in a wide arc, raising it as high as you can without raising your elbows, which should remain close to the body, contract fully at the top of the movement, then lower the weight slowly controlling it all the way down, do not swing the body or the weight during the curl movement.

PREACHER CURL (No.16)

The Muscles:- Biceps, Brachialis, Brachioradials

The Movements:- Position yourself with your chest against a Preacher Bench and extend your arm over it with a dumbell in your hand. Curl the weight up and flex your biceps at the top, then lower the weight slowly making sure you feel a complete stretch at the bottom of the movement. You can also do this with a barbell as pictured here.

CLOSE GRIP BENCH PRESS (No.17)

The Muscles:- Triceps

The Movements:- Grip the bar above the chest hands about six inches apart. Lift off the rack and hold with arms at full length. Now lower the bar to the chest slowly and press up again, slowly flexing the biceps with the elbows out and slightly forward. Do not bounce the bar off the chest.

LYING TRICEPS EXTENSION (No.18)

The Muscles:- Triceps

The Movements:- Lie on your back with your hand just off the end of the bench. Your knees should be bent with your feet flat on the bench. Grip a barbell with hands about 10" apart and press the bar up and out, until your arms are locked, with the weight back behind the top of your head. Keeping your elbows in place lower the weight down to your forehead slowly, then press it back up to the starting position.

CRUNCHES (No.19)

The Muscles:- Upper and Lower Abdominals

The Movements:- Lie flat on your back with your knees bent and place your hands by the side of your ears. Now curl yourself up, flexing your abdominals as tighly as you can, then lower yourself back down to the floor. Do not use your hands to make the movement easier and don't come all the way up to your knees. This exercise can also be done in reverse by bringing the knees to the shoulders.

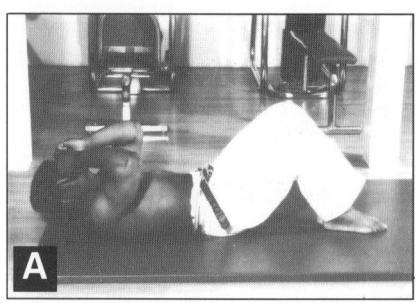 

SIDE CRUNCHES (No.20)
The Muscles:- Obliques, Abdominals
The Movements:- Lie on your right side with your knees slightly bent to stabilise your position. Your weight should rest on your gluteous muscles. Place your left hand by your ear, and your right hand on your left side. Now lie back to stretch the muscle and then using the muscles in your mid-section, curl yourself upwards and flex, then lower slowly. Then do this exercise on the reverse side.

WRIST CURL (No.21)
The Muscles:- Flexor Carpi Radialis
The Movements:- Grasp a barbell with an underhand grip, hands close together. Sit straddled on a bench, resting your forearms on the bench, with your wrists and hands hanging over the bench end. Now let the weight roll down as you bend your wrist down and open your fingers so that the weight is near the ends. Curl the weight up, bringing your wrist up and contract your forearm as hard as you can, release and start again.

REVERSE WRIST CURL (No.22)
The Muscles:- Extensor Carpi Ulnaris
The Movements:- Grasp a barbell with an overhand grip, hands about 8" apart and rest the forearms on the bench end. With wrists and hands unsupported, bend your wrists forwards and lower the bar as far as you can, then bring them back up and raise the bar, contracting the forearms. Try not to let the forearms move during this exercise.

TRAINING PROGRAMME

The following weight training programme has been specially formulated with the **martial artist** in mind. The exact weight to begin with depends entirely on the condition and strength of the individual and **advice should be taken** from a qualified gym instructor. The golden rule being: **start light and gradually build up as strength develops.** All 22 exercises demonstrated in the previous 8 pages are included.

EXERCISE	SETS	REPETITIONS			
		1st	2nd	3rd	4th
CHEST					
Flat Bench Press (No.1)	4	12	10	10	8
Incline Dumbell Press (No.2)	3	10	10	10	–
Flat Flys (No.3)	3	10	10	10	–
BACK					
Wide Grip Pulldown (No.4)	4	12	12	12	10
Seated Pulley Rows (No.5)	3	10	10	10	–
Isolating Dumbell Rows (No.6)	3 left & right	10	10	10	–
SHOULDERS					
Behind Neck Press (No.7)	3	10	10	10	–
Lateral Raises (No.8)	3	10	10	10	–
Reverse Flys (No.9)	3	10	10	10	–
Shrugs (No.10)	3	15	15	15	–
LEGS					
Squats (No.11)	4	15	12	10	10
Leg Extensions (No.12)	3	12	12	12	–
Leg Curl (No.13)	3	15	12	12	–
Standing Calf Raises (No.14)	3	MAXIMUM			
BICEPS					
Barbell Curl (No.15)	3	12	10	8	–
Preacher Curl (No.16)	3	10	10	10	–
TRICEPS					
Close Grip Bench Press (No.17)	3	12	10	10	–
Lying Triceps Extension (No.18)	3	12	10	10	–
MIDSECTION					
Crunches (No.19)	3	15	MAXIMUM		
Side Crunches (No.20)	3	10	MAXIMUM		
FOREARMS					
Wrist Curl (No.21)	3	MAXIMUM			
Reverse Wrist Curl (No.22)	3	MAXIMUM			

TRAINING ROUTINE

This routine allows for 3 training sessions over a 7 day period.

MONDAY	CHEST
	BICEPS
	FOREARMS (1 exercise)
	ABDOMINALS
WEDNESDAY	BACK
	TRICEPS
	FOREARMS (1 exercise)
	ABDOMINALS
FRIDAY	LEGS
	SHOULDERS
	ABDOMINALS

Anatomical Charts of Human Musculature
Front

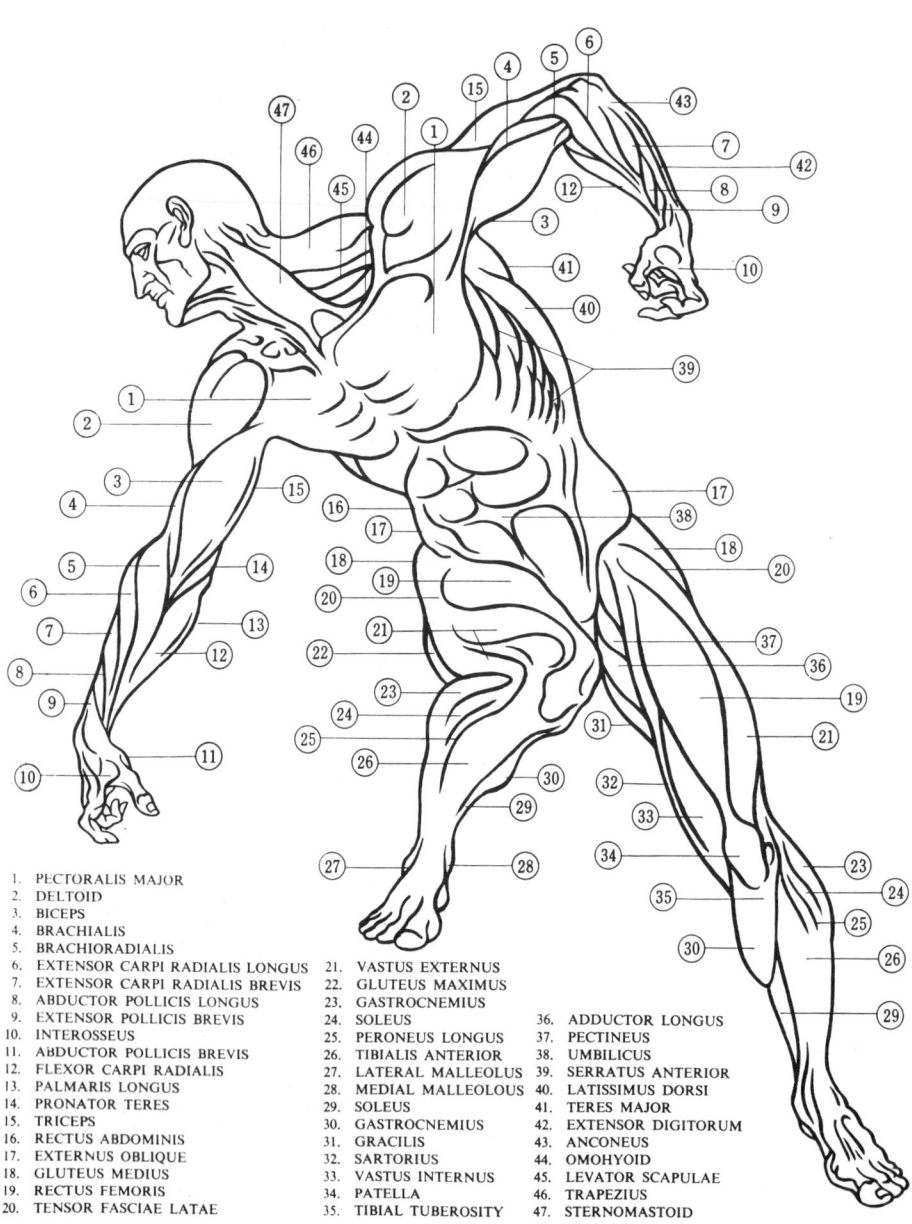

1. PECTORALIS MAJOR
2. DELTOID
3. BICEPS
4. BRACHIALIS
5. BRACHIORADIALIS
6. EXTENSOR CARPI RADIALIS LONGUS
7. EXTENSOR CARPI RADIALIS BREVIS
8. ABDUCTOR POLLICIS LONGUS
9. EXTENSOR POLLICIS BREVIS
10. INTEROSSEUS
11. ABDUCTOR POLLICIS BREVIS
12. FLEXOR CARPI RADIALIS
13. PALMARIS LONGUS
14. PRONATOR TERES
15. TRICEPS
16. RECTUS ABDOMINIS
17. EXTERNUS OBLIQUE
18. GLUTEUS MEDIUS
19. RECTUS FEMORIS
20. TENSOR FASCIAE LATAE

21. VASTUS EXTERNUS
22. GLUTEUS MAXIMUS
23. GASTROCNEMIUS
24. SOLEUS
25. PERONEUS LONGUS
26. TIBIALIS ANTERIOR
27. LATERAL MALLEOLUS
28. MEDIAL MALLEOLOUS
29. SOLEUS
30. GASTROCNEMIUS
31. GRACILIS
32. SARTORIUS
33. VASTUS INTERNUS
34. PATELLA
35. TIBIAL TUBEROSITY

36. ADDUCTOR LONGUS
37. PECTINEUS
38. UMBILICUS
39. SERRATUS ANTERIOR
40. LATISSIMUS DORSI
41. TERES MAJOR
42. EXTENSOR DIGITORUM
43. ANCONEUS
44. OMOHYOID
45. LEVATOR SCAPULAE
46. TRAPEZIUS
47. STERNOMASTOID

348

Back

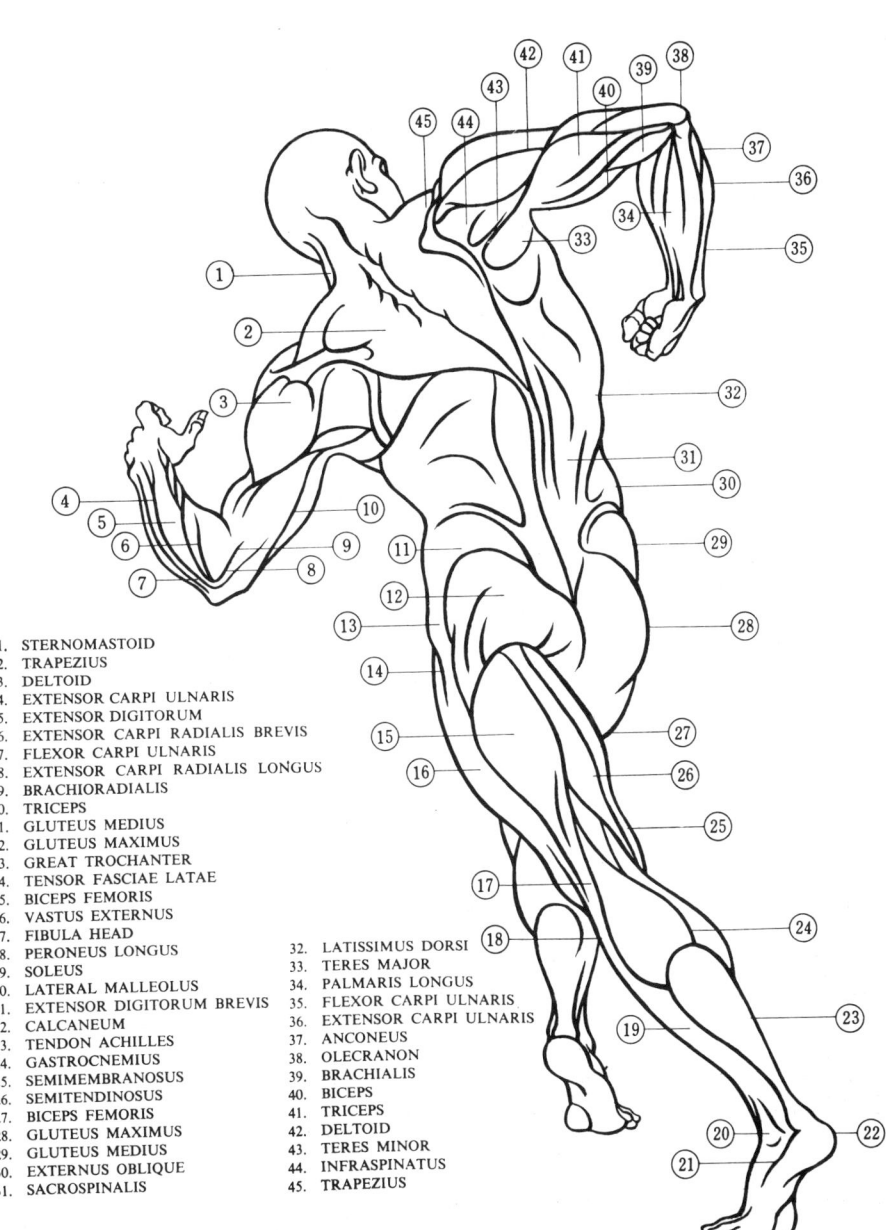

1. STERNOMASTOID
2. TRAPEZIUS
3. DELTOID
4. EXTENSOR CARPI ULNARIS
5. EXTENSOR DIGITORUM
6. EXTENSOR CARPI RADIALIS BREVIS
7. FLEXOR CARPI ULNARIS
8. EXTENSOR CARPI RADIALIS LONGUS
9. BRACHIORADIALIS
10. TRICEPS
11. GLUTEUS MEDIUS
12. GLUTEUS MAXIMUS
13. GREAT TROCHANTER
14. TENSOR FASCIAE LATAE
15. BICEPS FEMORIS
16. VASTUS EXTERNUS
17. FIBULA HEAD
18. PERONEUS LONGUS
19. SOLEUS
20. LATERAL MALLEOLUS
21. EXTENSOR DIGITORUM BREVIS
22. CALCANEUM
23. TENDON ACHILLES
24. GASTROCNEMIUS
25. SEMIMEMBRANOSUS
26. SEMITENDINOSUS
27. BICEPS FEMORIS
28. GLUTEUS MAXIMUS
29. GLUTEUS MEDIUS
30. EXTERNUS OBLIQUE
31. SACROSPINALIS

32. LATISSIMUS DORSI
33. TERES MAJOR
34. PALMARIS LONGUS
35. FLEXOR CARPI ULNARIS
36. EXTENSOR CARPI ULNARIS
37. ANCONEUS
38. OLECRANON
39. BRACHIALIS
40. BICEPS
41. TRICEPS
42. DELTOID
43. TERES MINOR
44. INFRASPINATUS
45. TRAPEZIUS

Body structure and vital points

Front

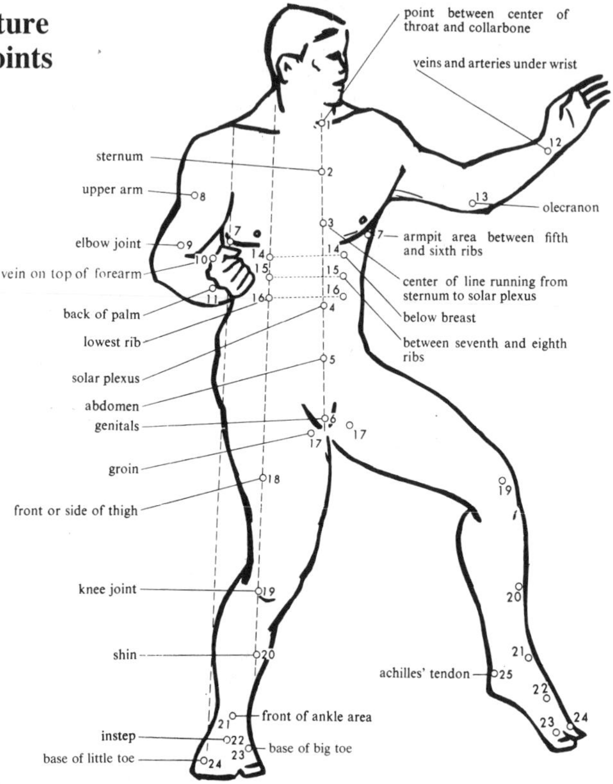

point between center of throat and collarbone
veins and arteries under wrist
sternum
upper arm
olecranon
elbow joint
armpit area between fifth and sixth ribs
vein on top of forearm
center of line running from sternum to solar plexus
back of palm
below breast
lowest rib
between seventh and eighth ribs
solar plexus
abdomen
genitals
groin
front or side of thigh
knee joint
shin
achilles' tendon
front of ankle area
instep
base of big toe
base of little toe

Where To Strike
and
What To Use

(*weapons*) (*strike points*)

▶ Face
knife hand 4–6, 8, 10–13
forefist 2–5, 9–11
inverted fist 3, 4, 7, 9
forefinger one-knuckle fist 3, 9, 11, 12
middle finger one-knuckle fist 3, 9, 11, 12
two-knuckle fist 4, 7, 11
dragon's head 3, 4, 9, 11, 12
spear hand 4, 9, 11, 12
forefinger spear 4
two-finger spear 4
chicken-beak hand 3, 4, 7
inner knife hand 5, 6, 8, 10, 13
palm heel 3, 4, 8–12
wrist 6, 8, 10, 12
fist edge 1, 2, 5, 6, 8, 10, 14
roundhouse kick 5, 6, 8, 10, 13

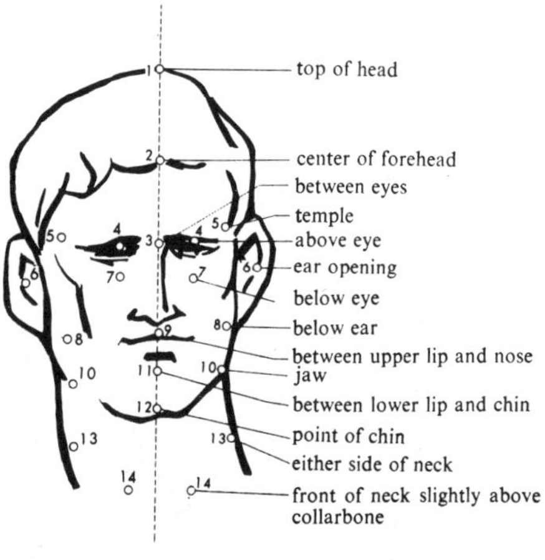

top of head
center of forehead
between eyes
temple
above eye
ear opening
below eye
below ear
between upper lip and nose
jaw
between lower lip and chin
point of chin
either side of neck
front of neck slightly above collarbone

The primary vital spots fall on a straight line midway in the human body and include the forehead, the upper lip, the solar plexus, and the genitals. The secondary vital points fall on straight lines centering on the temples and include the spots below the ears and the spots below the armpits. The tertiary vital spots fall on two lines midway between the primary line and the two secondary lines and include the ribs, spleen, and abdomen.

Back

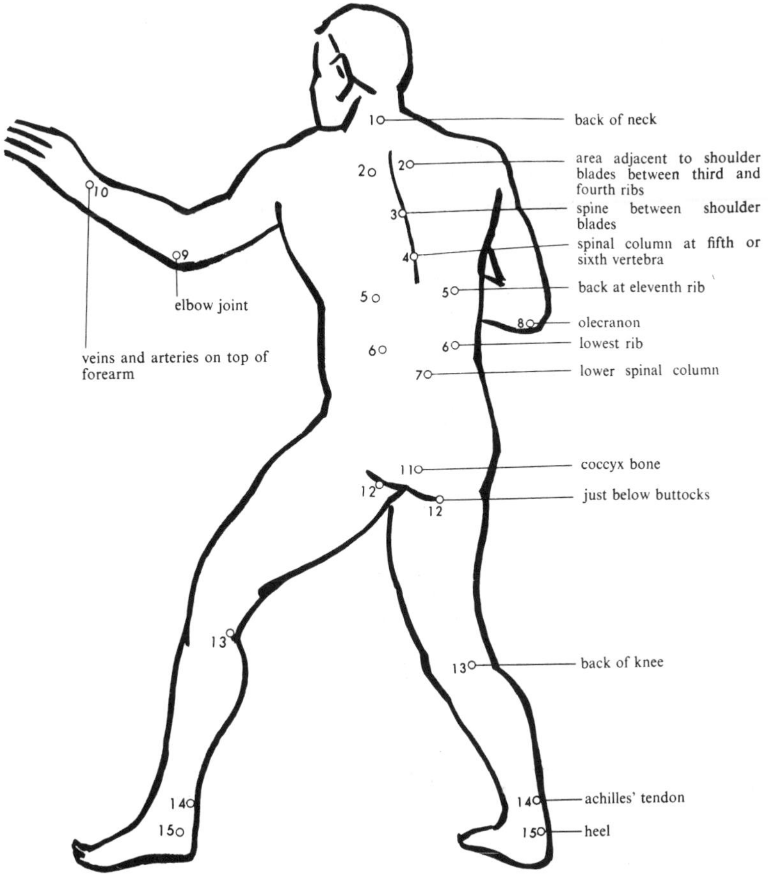

back of neck

area adjacent to shoulder blades between third and fourth ribs

spine between shoulder blades

spinal column at fifth or sixth vertebra

back at eleventh rib

olecranon

lowest rib

lower spinal column

elbow joint

veins and arteries on top of forearm

coccyx bone

just below buttocks

back of knee

achilles' tendon

heel

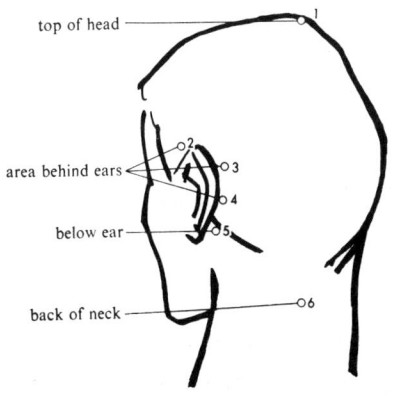

top of head

area behind ears

below ear

back of neck

WHERE TO STRIKE
AND
WHAT TO USE

(weapons) *(strike points)*

▶ Front view
knife hand   7, 14–16
forefist   2–7
inverted fist   3, 4, 7, 14–16
forefinger one-knuckle fist   1, 4
middle finger one-knuckle fist   1, 4
dragon's head   1
spear hand   1, 3, 4
forefinger spear   1, 3, 4
two-finger spear   1, 3, 4
inner knife hand   1, 7
palm heel   3–7
wrist   7, 14–16
fist edge   7, 14–16
roundhouse kick   1, 7, 14–16

knee kick   1, 6, 8, 17
front kick   3–6, 14–16
ankle kick   19, 21
heel   21–24
knife foot   4, 5, 6, 14–16

▶ Back view
knife hand   1
forefist   1, 5, 6
elbow   1–6
wrist   1–7
roundhouse kick,   5–7
front kick   11, 12

▶ Back of head
forefist   2–6
inverted fist   2–6
wrist   2–5
fist edge   1–6

351

CALISTHENICS AND EXERCISES

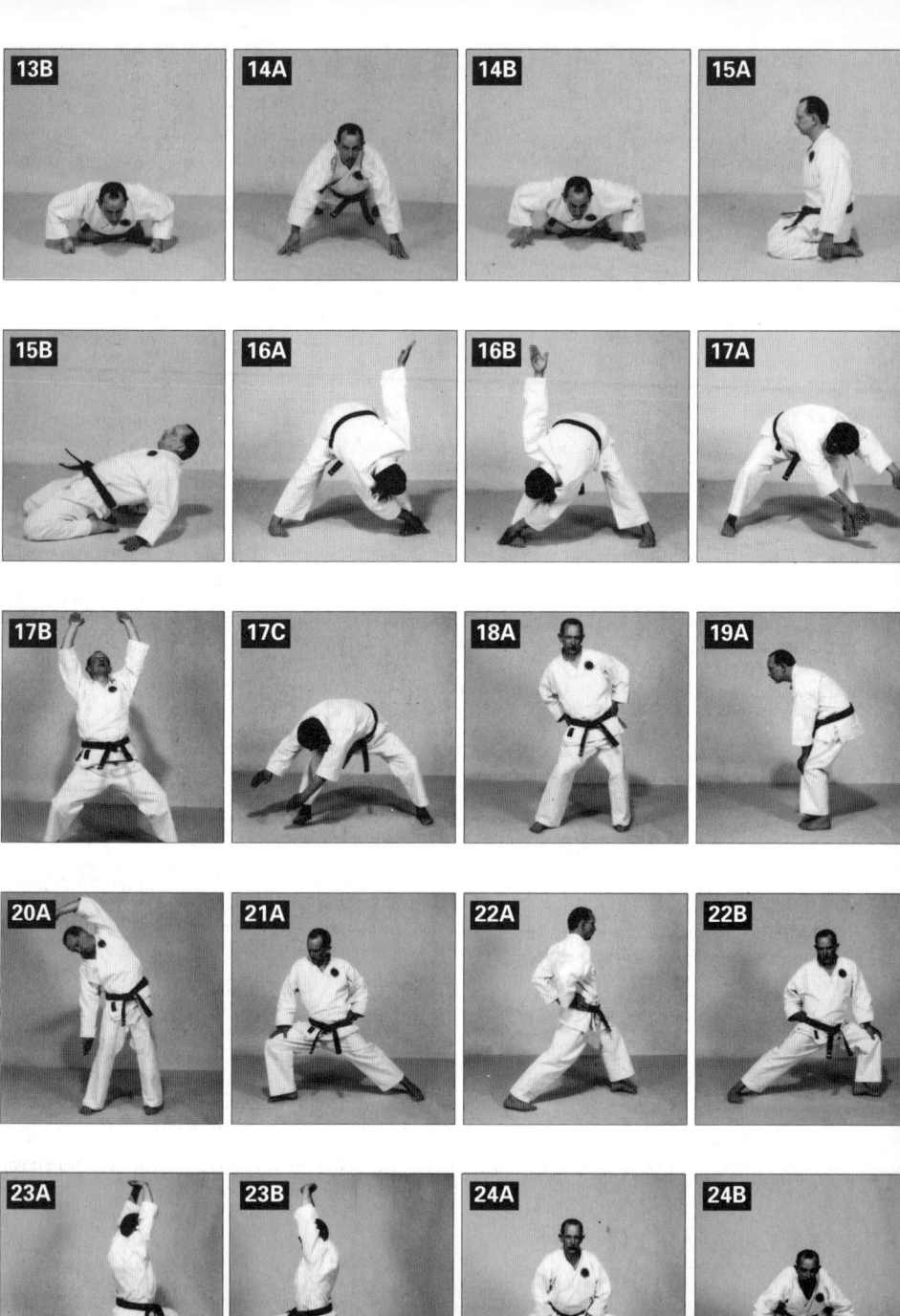

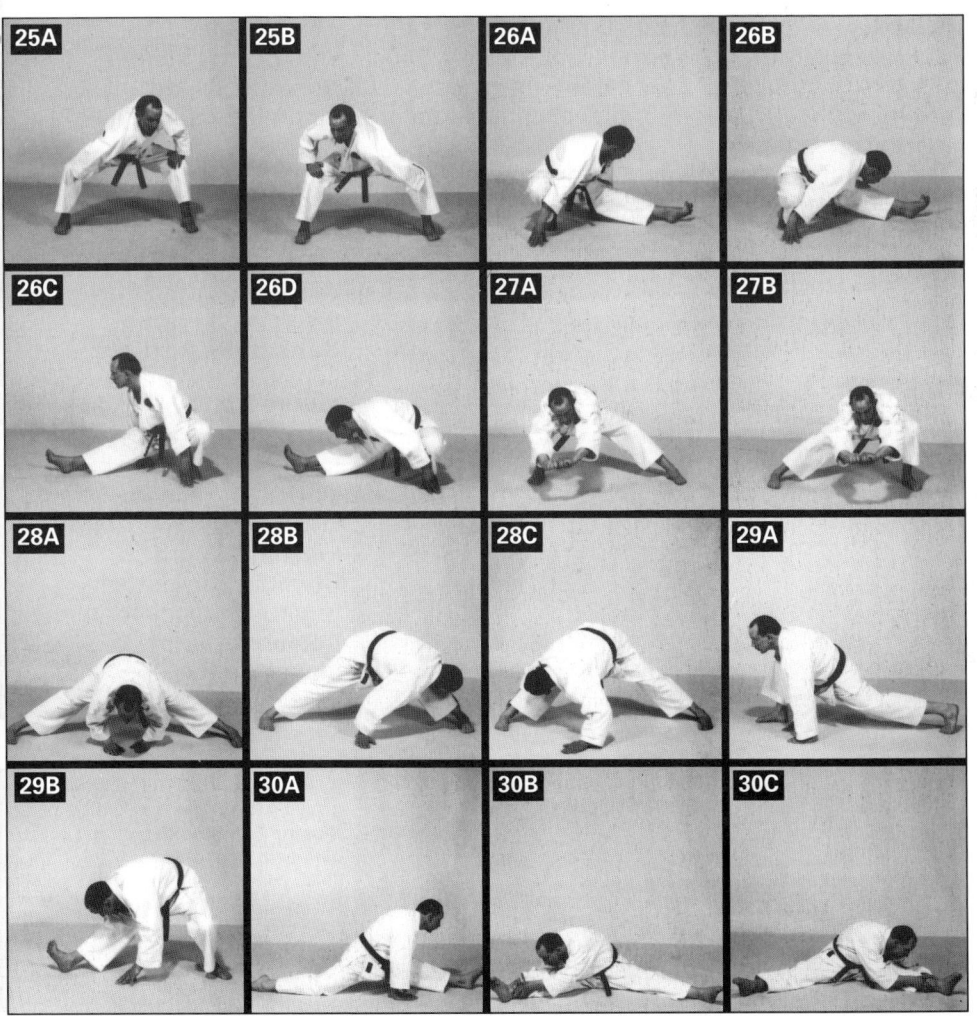

MASATOSHI NAKAYAMA

(1913 - 1987)

Nakayama Sensei, 9th dan, The Second Grand Master of the J.K.A., who inherited the Shotokan mantle from **Funakoshi Sensei,** was simultaneously a traditional Martial artist and a disciple of change. Under his leadership, the J.K.A. syllabus was enlarged and refined. New kicking techniques were introduced, as were a new dan structure leading to 9th dan, and an increasing emphasis on kumite practice. In addition, **Nakayama Sensei** presided over the international expansion of Shotokan karate. Tight organisation within Japan, and an enlightened mixture of control and automony for overseas J.K.A. branches, meant the growth of Shotokan until it became a major actor on the international martial arts stage.

The mixture of control and autonomy for overseas branches gave masters such as **Enoeda Sensei** the support and freedom to build strong and distinctive national bodies. At the same time, it also reflected

an essential division of labour within the J.K.A. **Nishiyama Sensei,** for instance, settled in the United States and, from there, led the **I.A.K.F.** in its rivalry with **W.U.K.O.,** and its current campaign with the International Olympic Committee regarding space for a traditional karate alongside the W.U.K.O. sports karate.

A rare photograph indeed and possibly the last ever taken of **Master Funakoshi**, pictured here with his successor **Nakayama Sensei**, in the spring of 1957, just prior to the master's death. Note the master's left hand is formed in **Nakadaka Ippon Ken.**

The international growth and organisation of Shotokan is **Nakayama Sensei's abiding legacy.** Whoever replaces him will have difficulty in replicating his judicious view of how to treat the several senior masters within the J.K.A. and the J.K.A.'s place among other international karate organisations. Time will reveal what a master of diplomacy and balance **Nakayama Sensei** was, in addition to his mastery of karate.

His open-mindedness has always informed his martial arts career. He interrupted his training under **Funakoshi Sensei** during World War II, spending the war years in **China.** There, he had the freedom to undertake solo explorations of **China,** and met many (what he called) **Chinese Kempo** teachers. Often, he was able to pass for Chinese having studied Chinese civilisation and language at Tokyo's **Takushoku University** (where he was later Professor of Physical Education). This gave him the insight into Chinese martial arts denied to his less prepared contempories. In the end **Nakayama Sensei** rejected what he called the Chinese emphasis on power built in a continuous arc, in favour of the kime or focus that became firmly identified with Shotokan.

My own experiences of training with **Nakayama Sensei** were at the old J.K.A. in Tokyo in 1967 – 1968. Together with **Eddie Whitcher** and **Mike Peachy,** I trained in the morning class, held every weekday, just prior to the instructors class. The lessons were taken on a rota basis by the senior J.K.A. instructors, and once a week **Nakayama Sensei** would take the class himself. His instruction was superb, and I always felt it a priviledge and great honour just to be in the same room as this man.

He always maintained the art was a vehicle for improving the character, and what was most important to understand, was that this seeking of better character was not a temporary or fleeting goal. It was a **life long process,** to be persued every day through training.

Nakayama Sensei recognised a pluralistic karate world and sought an ecumenical-style agreement within it. Certainly, in his later years of instruction, his teaching style differed radically from the tough and harshly competitive drills of **Takushoku University** – being far more thoughtful and inward-looking. In this sense, he was not only the leader of the J.K.A., but the mature restraining factor on tendencies within it. There was room for extremes of practice, provided they did not overwhelm the true meaning of karate.

With the death of **Nakayama Sensei,** the karate world, not just the Shotokan world, has lost a major and magnificent figure – a pioneer and a statesman. Shotokan practitioners will remember him in their own way. For other Karateka, there may be a different view of what were his major accomplishments, **but there will be agreement that a great debt was owed to him and that, with his death, a chapter of karate's history has closed.**

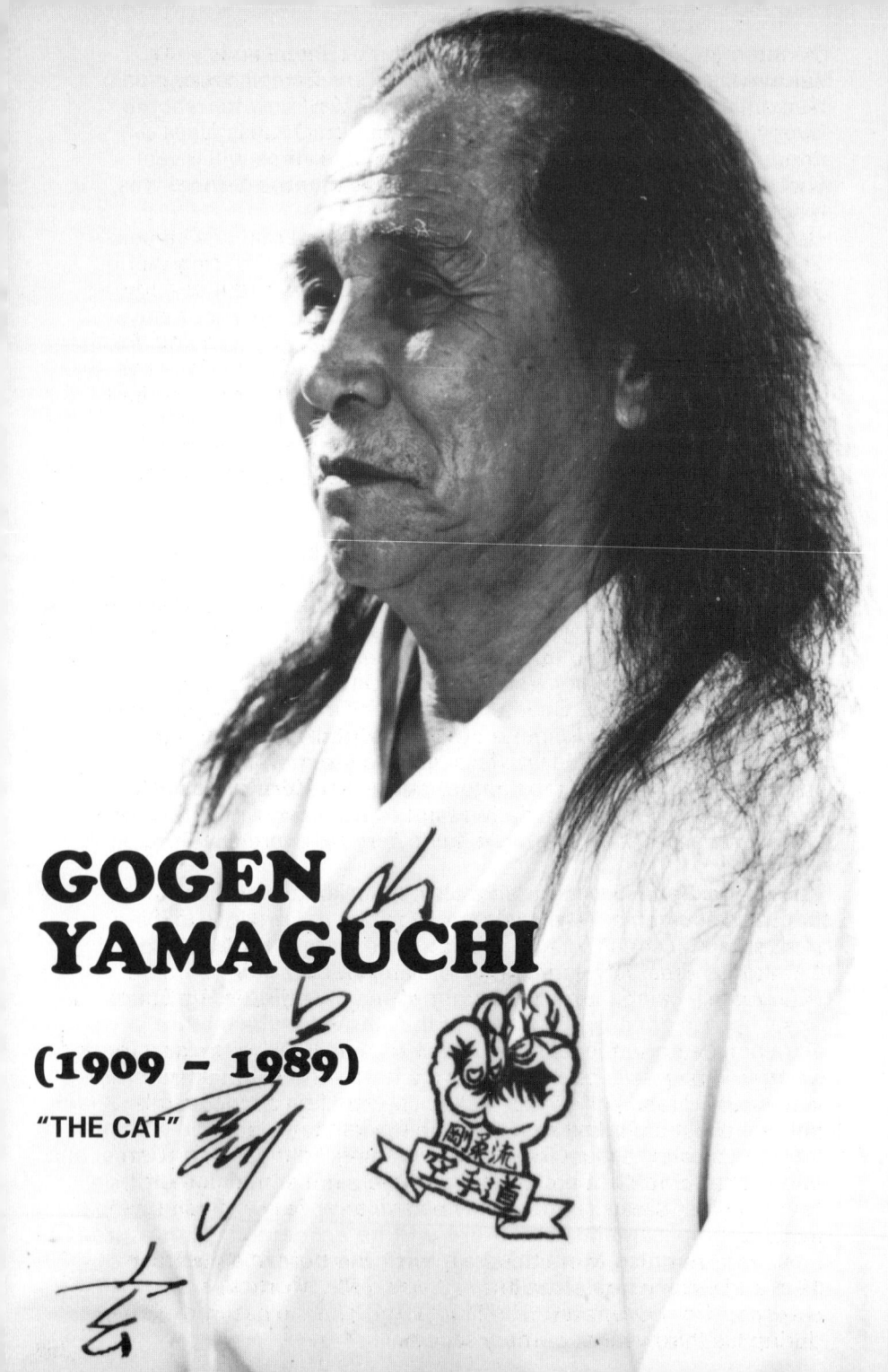

GOGEN YAMAGUCHI

(1909 – 1989)

"THE CAT"

During my years in Australia, I read with avid interest virtually every article that had ever been written about **Gogen Yamaguchi Sensei,** or as he was better known – **"The Cat".**

Most of the time, **Yamaguchi Sensei** wore traditional Japanese dress and with his long flowing black hair, looked every inch a Samurai Warrior, and to most, had become a legend in his own time. I was no exception.

One day in December 1967, I was winding my way through the **Tokyo** streets in the suburb of **Ichigaya,** heading for **Yotsuya** Station, where I would catch the Chuo line to **Korakuen** and the J.K.A. Dojo. By 9.30 a.m., I had crossed the main highway, and taken the little path that ran alongside the canal. Approaching the station, I bought a ticket and walked onto the platform just as the train pulled alongside me. Deep in thought over the previous days lesson, I boarded the subway train and sat down. I remember looking at the floor and going through **Bassai Dai** in my mind. When I had finished the Kata, I brought my head up, and looked across to the other side of the carriage.

I froze. Sitting only six feet in front of me, with his long flowing black hair and black Kimono, observing me intently was **"The Cat" Gogen Yamaguchi.** I reacted by going into a state of shock, to which he gave me a warm smile and beckoned me to come and sit with him. He spoke no English and I very little Japanese, but somehow we managed to communicate.

The following Saturday, was to be a special day in the Karate world, for an All Styles Championships between **East Japan and West Japan** was to take place at **The Budokan** and **Yamaguchi Sensei** was to be the Guest of Honour. He insisted I should go with him as **his** guest. I was dumbfounded. At **Korakuen,** I left the train, but not before initiating the deepest bow ever to **Sensei** and with a promise to meet him the following Saturday at 7.00 p.m.

I arrived just after 6.00 p.m. and waited outside the main entrance for **Sensei** to come. **The Budokan** was filled to capacity and I noticed people were being turned away. Precisely at 7.00 p.m. **Sensei** arrived. I felt terribly nervous and wondered if he would even remember the chance meeting with the **Gaijin** on the Chuo line.

To my absolute astonishment, he smiled broadly when he saw me and gestured that I should walk alongside him. Quite suddenly we were in the Arena and I dropped back behind him as thousands of people rose to their feet to give him a standing ovation.

Hours later, after a most memorable evening, I left the **Budokan** and walked home through the busy Tokyo streets. At times it all seemed like a dream, but I knew it wasn't and I felt very honoured indeed.

I had read so much about this man, who was born in **Kyushu** in 1909 and was one of ten children. It was a **Mr. Maruta,** a carpenter from **Okinawa** who first taught him the basics of Karate during his third year at primary school.

In 1931 at the age of 22, **Gogen Yamaguchi** met **Chojun Miyagi** for the first time and began training with him. In the late 1930's and early 1940's, he worked for the Japanese Government as an administrator in **Manchuria.** With the ending of World War II in 1945, he was unfortunately captured by the Russians and detained in a labour camp. Two years later, in 1947, he was released and repatriated.

He became the most senior student of **Goju Ryu** in Japan and is the man credited for being directly responsible for the growth of **Goju Ryu** karate in Japan. His first dojo opened in 1948, and in May 1950, he established **"The All Japan Karate Dō Goju Kai".** In due course, he formulated his own system of **Goju Shintō,** a **combination** of **Goju style Karate, Yoga, Shintō** and **Zen.** He was fully versed in Shinto rituals and familiar with various Yogas, **Hatha Yoga, Raja Yoga** and **Kundalini Yoga.** He based his understanding of the human body on **Yoga physiology** and its seven **Chakras.** He defined **Goju Ryu** as **"Seishin No Mono",** a thing of the spirit and in the early 1970's founded his **"Japan Karate do College"** located in Tokyo's **Suginami** suburb.

In 1989, **Gogen Yamaguchi Sensei** died, and the karate world mourned his passing. At his funeral in Tokyo, every style and country were represented. As I write these words in 1995, my real thoughts are back there, 28 years ago, to a certain railway carriage, and a Karate Master who offered **The Hand of Friendship** to a rather lonely and insignificant foreigner.

MORIO HIGAONNA

It was a great priviledge for me to train under **Higaonna Sensei** recently when he presided over an Open Course at Crystal Palace in London. **Higaonna Sensei** is now resident in the U.S.A. and is **Chief Instructor to the International Okiniwan Goju-Ryu Karate-dō Federation.**

Like all Great Karate Masters, he exudes humility. Being the only Shotokan Student on the course, I felt rather conspicious, due to my total lack of knowledge of **Goju-Ryu** but within minutes of commencing training, he made me feel very much at home. I couldn't help feeling a little embarassed at the end of the course when **he** thanked **me** for coming. As I left Crystal Palace, it was with a feeling of the utmost admiration for **Higaonna Sensei.** I had read in books of **Higaonna Sensei's** devotion to his personal teacher **Anichi Miyagi Sensei** and in turn, his relationship with his teacher, **Chojun Miyagi Sensei.** If **Higaonna Sensei's** impeccable behaviour was anything to go by, I sure would have liked to have met his teachers teacher **Chojun Miyagi Sensei** the Founder of **Goju-Ryu Karate.**

"The author with Higaonna Sensei"

MASUTATSU OYAMA

(1923 – 1994)

The author (right) with Masutatsu Oyama at the Kyokushinkai headquarters in Tokyo in 1967.

Sosai Oyama was born in South West Korea and first went to Japan in 1938 at the age of 15. A year later, he began karate training with **Funakoshi Sensei** and within 3 to 4 years, was awarded Shodan.

At the end of the war, **Sosai Oyama** left civilisation behind and retreated to **Mount Kiyozumi** in Chiba Prefecture, where he remained in isolation for 18 months. During that time, he hunted animals for food, practised meditation and trained incredibly hard every day.

A powerful and charismatic figure, **Sosai Oyama** founded **The Kyokushinkai** in 1956. Broken down, the word **Kyokushinkai** means: **Kyoku** – The final meaning of life, **Shin** – heart, and **Kai** – Association. From those humble beginnings, **The Kyokushinkai** today has over 10 million members world-wide.

I first read Sosai's books **"What is Karate"** and later **"This is Karate"**, whilst I was a kyu grade in **South Australia** in 1964 – 1965. He became a hero figure to me and I wrote to him in **Japan** to ask if he would accept me as a student. I didn't expect a reply and I was quite astounded when an airmail letter arrived in Adelaide, with an invitation to go to **Tokyo** and **train at his dojo!**

Five years later, I walked into his dojo at **Ikebukuro,** clutching my blue airmail letter. He made me so welcome, introduced me to many of his instructors, most of whom, were at that time, working on the latest James Bond film, **"You Only Live Twice"**, with Sean Connery. That night, I was his guest at a new Korean Restaurant he had recently opened, close to the dojo and his hospitality was overwhelming.

Although I returned to see him many times, I never did train at his dojo, as I had met **Kanazawa Sensei** and was training at the J.K.A. **Sosai Oyama** spoke highly of **Nakayama Sensei,** and I corresponded with him for many years.

Sosai Oyama was the most charismatic man I have ever met. He had an amazing presence, and when I heard of his death in April 1994 – **a part of me died too.**

KARATE vs CANCER 1990

There comes a time in most people's lives when they have a desire to "put something back". "Where" and "how" is often more difficult to answer and the necessary motivation is not always forthcoming. That motivation manifested itself in no uncertain terms in the form of Eddie Whitcher.

Eddie, who had pioneered Shotokan Karate in Great Britain in the early 'sixties was suffering from terminal cancer. Throughout his karate life he had been an inspiration to all. Big in stature and mild in manner he was without doubt an extremely gifted Shotokan Traditionalist. A purist in the true sense of the word seeking neither material gain nor recognition.

Visiting him at the Royal London Hospital with Kanazawa Sensei in November 1989, I was shocked by his frail gaunt appearance. As fellow students in 1967, I had watched him fight the best the J.K.A. had to offer – and beat them. Alas – how could he have known the real enemy would come from within.

Happier times: Eddie Whitcher, the family man. Relaxing at home in early 1988.

KARATE vs CANCER 1990

Professor Williams of the Medical Unit at the Royal London Hospital was in charge of his treatment. He did everything in his power to save Eddie's life – sadly, he failed and I couldn't help but be aware of the frustration being experienced by the medical unit due to lack of finance to fund much needed research into finding a cure for this terrible disease.

It was with much pride that I announced to Professor Williams that the members of T.A.S.K. had unanimously agreed to support his research and a target of £50,000 had been set.

So began the biggest ever fundraising event in martial arts history and "Karate vs Cancer" was born. It would span 9 months and culminate on 30th September 1990 with a massive display of punching at T.A.S.K.'s hombu in Bedford.

Martial artists from up and down the country responded magnificently and special thanks went to S.K.A. and E.S.K.A.

Three proud instructors of the clubs who raised the most money.
1st (centre) Stamford, 2nd (left) Flitwick, 3rd (right) Luton.

KARATE vs CANCER 1990

As the 30th September 1990 drew to a close, it was fitting that Eddie Whitcher's two children, Clinton and Camille, should present Professor Williams with a cheque for £125,000.

In his reply, Professor Norman Williams said: "Eddie Whitcher was a remarkable man. He bore his illness with great courage and fortitude. He brought joy to the people looking after him. His inner strength and his superb family helped him cope."

A special guest was 12-year-old James Wightman who's greatest wish was to do karate. James, who had a tumour on the brain, here receives an honorary black belt from Sensei Van Weenen. Two days earlier, James had become blind and Sensei said, "He's the most courageous boy I've ever known". Sadly, a few days later, he died.

KARATE vs CANCER 1990

The final total exceeded the original target 3 times and stands at £158,000.

In the eyes of many of the general public, karate remains just a shade less than respectable, with very little being known of the philosophy concerning "The Way". My sincere hope is that this small effort will have gone some way in redressing the balance and in the process, the image of karate will become a little less tarnished.

Clinton Whitcher (left) and his sister Camille, just prior to presenting the Royal London Hospital with a cheque for £125,000.

Over £4,000 was raised for the widow and children of Eddie Whitcher on a special course put on by seven of his friends.

100 black belts pose for this memorable photograph behind instructors (left to right), Mick Randall, John van Weenen, Mick Nursey, Roger Hall, Harry Jones, Greg Durant and Neville Whitfield.

Taken at Luton in September 1977, H. Kanazawa then 8th Dan, performs his famous butterfly kick after being attacked by E. Whitcher 4th Dan (right) and J. van Weenen 2nd Dan (left).

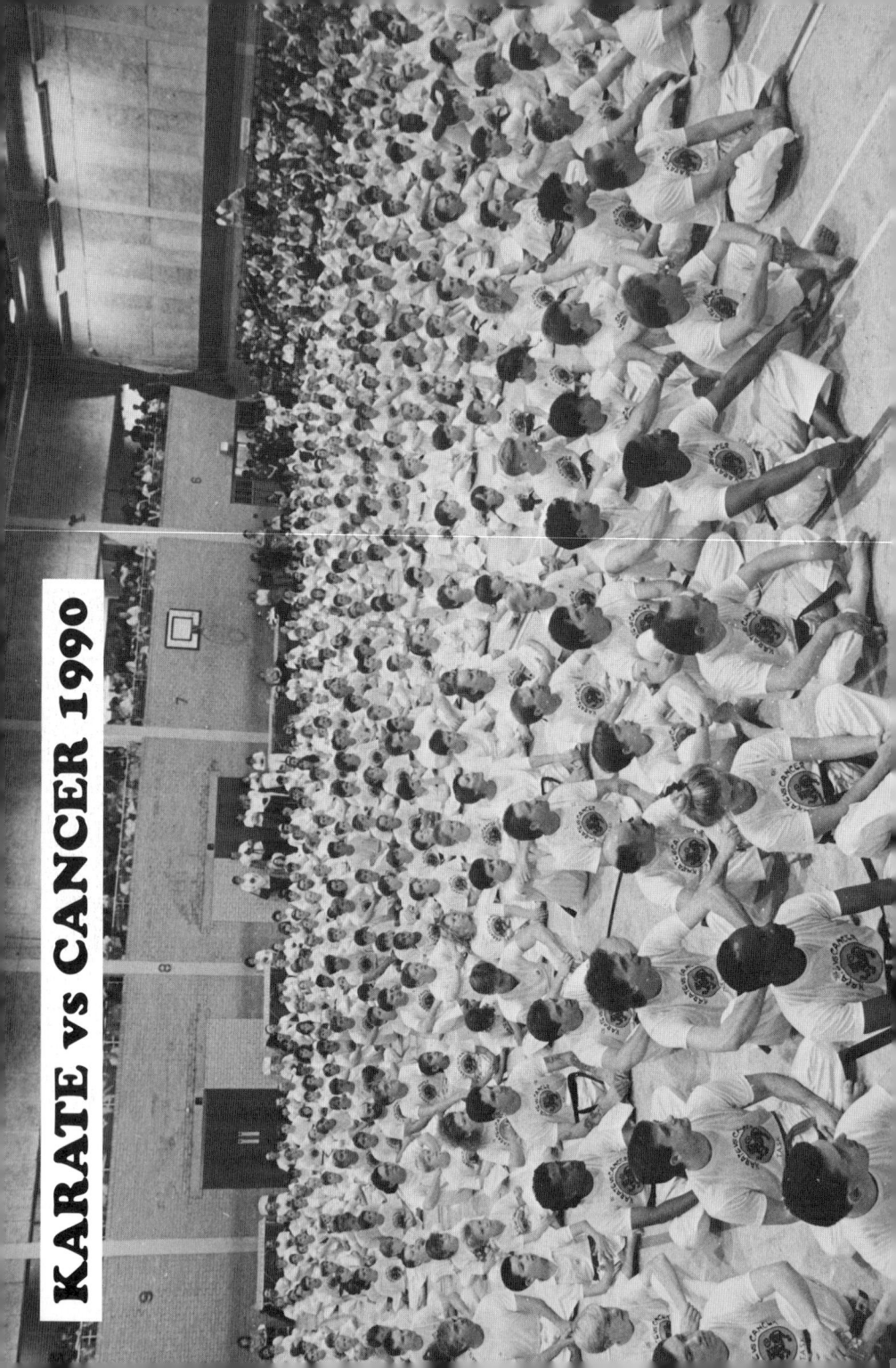

KARATE vs CANCER 1990

A few months before his death Gichin Funakoshi wrote:

"Today, almost everywhere in Japan, I can hear the voices of karate training.
Now, finally, karate has been introduced to far places abroad. As I look back over the past forty years to those days in the beginning when I was first introducing karate with my friends, it is indeed difficult for me to grasp the present widespread acceptance of karate. It seems as if it were a different period."

Throughout his life, Funakoshi Sensei preached and taught traditional values.

I am sure he would take great comfort in knowing they were being adhered to thirty-three years after his death. What finer tribute to him could there be, than for 1,000 of his third generation students to come together, on the other side of the world, motivated, as indeed he was, by nothing more than a desire to help their fellow man.

A fine shot of Sensei Mick Randall (left) performing Jodan Mawashi Geri as the late Sensei Eddie Whitcher counters simultaneously with Yoko Geri Kekomi. This photograph was taken in 1980 when both men were joint Chief Instructors of E.S.K.A.

TASK FORCE
ALBANIA

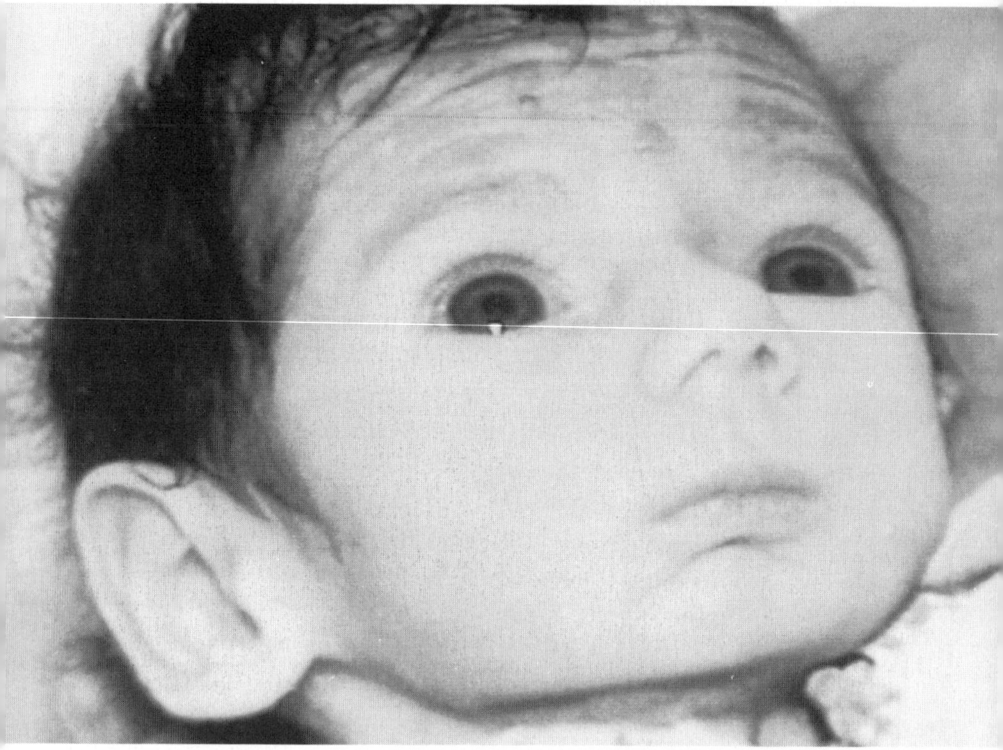

On the 21st September 1991, the image of a tiny malnourished Albanian girl was shown on British television for the first time. The picture, taken by Bhasker Solanki and Bill Hamilton of the BBC, had quite an incredible effect on the British people and in particular, the author of this book. By the time **Jessica's** story had reached our television screens, she was already **dead**, weighing at five months one pound less than her birth weight.

Two weeks later, I was leaving Heathrow bound for Tirana, the capital of Albania and it would be the Albanian Democratic Party Leader, Dr. Sali Berisha, who would meet me at Rhinas Airport. During the next seven days, he showed me his country and his people, still dominated as they had been for fifty years by Communism, most of it under the tyrannical dictatorship of Enver Hoxha.

Returning to England, determined to do something, I enlisted the help of T.A.S.K. The members responded immediately and within days, the new charity **"Task Force Albania"** was formed and a campaign to transport aid to Albania quickly gathered momentum.

Three months later, after having set up collection points in over **100 towns and cities** in the U.K., the largest single convoy ever assembled in peace time, departed on 26th January 1992 from Bedford.

The President of Albania, Dr. Sali Berisha with the author.

It comprised of twenty thirty-eight tonne juggernauts, carrying over **seven hundred tonnes** of food, clothing and medical supplies to Europe's poorest country.

The trip, although extremely hazardous, was tremendously successful with **95%** of all the aid reaching the Albanian people. The support team of thirty T.A.S.K. students and instructors were superb and played a major role in achieving our objectives.

In March 1992, the Democratic Party won a landslide victory over the Communists and their leader, **Dr. Sali Berisha**, became the President of Albania.
Now the real work could begin and I felt an irresistible compulsion to play a very small part in bringing Albania into the 20th century.

Hospital conditions were appalling and the health service under the Communists had been decimated. Doctors and surgeons like all other Albanian nationals were forbidden to travel abroad, resulting in a tremendous thirst for western knowledge. The course of action was obvious.

Suppose I could bring some of the best English doctors to Albania and vice versa. At that time, it all seemed somewhat ambitious with the problems of language, communication, visas, passports and finance to be overcome. Charles Hutton, director of the New Victoria hospital in Kingston-Upon-Thames, London, responded magnificently, as did surgeon Nick Jacobs, anaesthetist John Maynard and O.D.A. John Gurrin.

The "New Victoria" team flew to Tirana in May 1992 at their own expense and successfully performed complicated eye surgery on **twenty orphaned children**, many of whom were blind or suffering from severe squints, cataracts and glaucoma.

Correspondingly, four months later, **"Task Force Albania"** brought three eminent doctors specialising in Pediatrics, Ophthalmology and Anaesthesia to London to study western technology at the top London teaching hospitals. So successful was it, that all three, on their return to Tirana, conducted seminars in their own field, attracting doctors from the length and breadth of Albania.

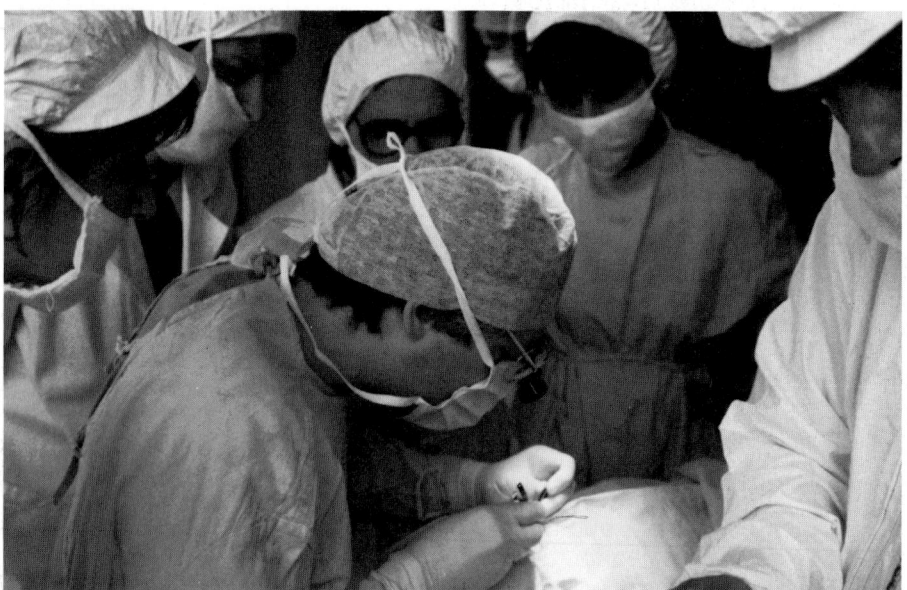

Dr. Nick Jacobs performing eye surgery in Tirana on Anila, a blind orphan girl.

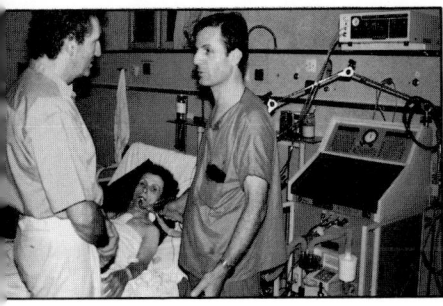

Dr. Roland Xhaxho on 18 June 1992 receiving Albania's first jet ventilator from John van Weenen. It arrived just in time to save Fatime Hasani's life, suffering from a collapsed lung condition.

Children from Shkodra's "Teufik G'yli" orphanage in their new clothes from England, are given "sweets" for the first time.

Huddled together on cold stone floors in their own excreta, were the children of Shkodra's mentally handicapped institute comforted to the best of her ability by Anila, aged 14, lice ridden and blind from birth.

A jubilant Prof. Sulejman Zhugli head of Tirana's ophthamological department, receiving Albania's first "Perimeter" brought from England by T.F.A.

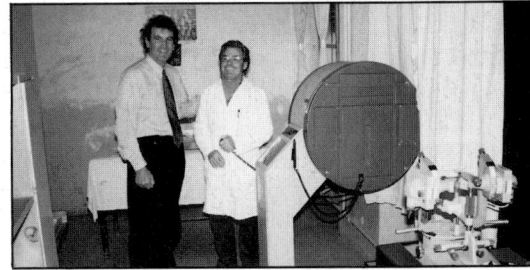

As she is today, pictured visiting England, thanks to a good samaritan, Mrs Barbara Locke.

"Task Force Albania" received official charity status in November 1992 and Esther Rantzen very kindly saw fit to include us in her BBC December **"Hearts of Gold"** television programme.

With Albania celebrating **"Christmas"** for the first time in fifty years, christians were jubilant to say the least and although in his infinite wisdom, Enver Hoxha had **"abolished God and Christianity"**, he failed to remove it from the hearts and minds of a vast number of people.

Fortunately, like **Edith Durham** the English anthropologist before me, I had developed a "fatal attraction" for "Malesia E Madhe". No aid whatsoever had gone to this part of northern Albania and its tribal people were desperate. Every truck we could muster, took much needed food, clothing and medical supplies to Bajze, Koplik, Tamara, Shkodra and Vermosh and every item was donated free of charge by the people of England.

The children of Kingsbrook Middle School in Bedford "loading up" their aid.

T.F.A. trucks arriving on Albanian soil at Durres after a long trip from Trieste by ferry.

Finally, the "well guarded" warehouse in Bajze.

In March 1993, Bedfordshire schoolchildren's campaign to clothe their Albanian counterparts received official backing from the Minister of Education **Baroness Blatch**. The children's generosity had to be seen to be believed, all started by pupils of Kingsbrook Middle School in Bedford.

Just prior to this, I had the wonderful opportunity to visit Calcutta to meet Albania's most famous citizen - **Mother Teresa**. No words can adequately express my admiration and respect for this tiny, frail 83 year old lady who arrived in 1937 in Entally, a suburb of Calcutta, with just **a five rupee note - and a lot of faith!** Never once asking for government backing or church funding, she has managed to build a vast network of missionaries of charity, over 600 in 108 countries worldwide. To the world's destitute, she gives **hope**. To the poor, afflicted and diseased she shows **love**. In these troubled times in which we live, she restores faith in human nature, without doubt - **a living saint**.

Talking to her in April 93, having just returned from the Great Highlands after delivering medical aid with the invaluable help of TASK members Alan Bristow, Azad Kumar and Alan Blake, I noticed she was troubled.

In June 1992, President Berisha bestowed upon John the nation's highest civilian honour, "The Order of Mother Teresa". He very proudly accepted it on behalf of all Karate-Ka from Albania's most famous citizen herself.

A major problem for her now that her organisation has grown so large, is getting from country to country. She has to rely totally on charity and as she never asks for it - it isn't **ALWAYS** forthcoming.

Perhaps I should have a word with British Airways on my return to London. "Would you really?" she replied. "That would be wonderful". I have to say, not knowing anyone at B.A. and starting from scratch, was a shade daunting but I was determined not to be fobbed off by an army of secretaries.

A week later, from executive level came the answer I had been hoping for. British Airways would provide Mother Teresa and her travelling companion with **FREE** 1st class tickets, to travel at will on any British Airways route, anywhere in the world, for the rest of her life. I thought to myself, "Mother will be pleased".

Gichin Funakoshi

Mother Teresa

The other day, whilst reading Funakoshi Sensei's **"Karate Dō Kyōhan"**, I came to the chapter entitled **"Maxims for the Trainee"**. Although I had read this piece many times before, a couple of lines seemed to take on a whole new meaning.

"Make benevolence your lifelong duty. This surely is an important mission. It is a lifelong effort, truly a long journey".

How strange I thought. In one sentence he had captured the whole meaning of **Karate Dō**, whilst epitomising the long struggle and unselfish dedication of a certain, **rather special, Loreto Nun.**

(0234) 363101. Fax: (0234) 325721

Prime Minister backs appeal for Albania

PRIME Minister John Major has given his backing to the TASK Force Albania mercy mission from Bedford following an appeal by co-ordinator John Van Weenan.

To summarize then, since October 1991, Task Force Albania have made **21Humanitarian Aid Missions** taking over **£5 million of aid** to Europe's poorest country, all of which has been donated free by the British people.

To help meet transportation costs, in recent months, the **Overseas Development Administration** have made two grants for which we are most grateful.

A brief synopsis of T.F.A.'s efforts now follows:

January 1992
(2nd Mission) 20 Juggernaut trucks leave Britain loaded with food and clothing. **The largest aid convoy** to leave Britain since World War 2.

April 1992
(3rd Mission) Visit to make all arrangements for arrival of **British Doctors** in Albania.

May 1992
(4th Mission) Team of Doctors fly to Albania to perform complicated eye surgery on **20 orphaned children.**

May 1992
(5th Mission) Aid to Orphanages in **Shkodra.**

June 1992
(6th Mission) **Jet ventilator** to Intensive Care Unit at Tirana Hospital. Request of Minister of Health.

September 1992
(7th Mission) Aid to Tirana and escort three leading **Albanian Doctors** to London.

October 1992
(8th Mission) Survey of all hospitals in the **Great Highlands of Albania.**

November 1992
(9th Mission) Aid to the Commune of **Bajze.**

January 1993
(10th Mission) Warm clothing and bedding to **Tirana Koplik** and **Bajze.**

April 1993
(11th Mission) Snow melts. Aid to the far north of Albania to the villages of **Tomara** and **Vermosh.**

July 1993
(12th Mission) Discussions and meetings in **Tirana.** Visit to **Vlora.**

September 1993
(13th Mission) 500 Rotary boxes to **Bajze.** Dentistry Equipment to **Koplik.**

THE TEAM

Azad Kumar

Alan Bristow

Alan Blake

Roy Richards

Michael Batten

Gordon Collis

Bernard Coppen

Bob Poynton

Michael Randall

October 1993
14th Mission) Aid to **Berat, Vlora, Shkodra** and villages in **Kruma** district.

November 1993
15th Mission) Three trucks including 500 Rotary boxes to warehouse in **Durres.** Aid from **Mother Teresa's** home in London to **Shkodra.**

February 1994
16th Mission) Empty warehouse in **Durres.** 12 Military trucks to **Shkodra** with 50% to northern villages.

May 1994
17th Mission) **Vermosh** and 10 villages of the **Kelmandi** Region with 1,000 Rotary boxes. Aid to Bajze School and Medical Centre.

September 1994
18th Mission) **£200,000 of Medical Equipment** to Tirana Hospital. **£40,000 of Educational Aid** to Koplik. Delivery of Mazda van.

November 1994
19th Mission) 1,000 Rotary boxes to **Thethe** and other villages. **£350,000 of Antibiotics** to Ministry in Tirana.

January 1995
20th Mission) Visit with Norman Wisdom. Exploratory talks with regard to building a medical clinic in **Tirana** in conjunction with four other British Charities – **Feed the Children, ADRA, Childhope and Jersey Aid.**

March 1995
21st Mission) 1000 boxes of clothing to **Librazsd** in central eastern Albania. Feasibility study under-taken to give assistance to 138,000 destitute people in 60 mountain villages.

Task Force Albania has also sent considerable consignments of aid to the following Cities, Towns and Villages:

Tirana; Shkodra; Kavaja; Bajze; Koplik; Kruma; Thethe; Tomara; Vermosh; Hani Hoti; Lepusha; Selca; Broja; Kozhnje; Vulke; Nikci; Bratoshe; Kastrat; Breglumi; Lotaj; Shoshi; Pulti; Sukaj; Boga; Dedaj and Vuksanaj.

In addition to this, a Pilot Scheme to supply Albania's top Surgeons with reliable **FOUR Wheel Drive Vehicles** got under way. The first vehicle arrived in October and **Professor Sulejman Zhugli,** Head of Albania's Ophthalmological Society took possession. It will enable him to visit outlying villages and hospitals to perform eye surgery whilst, at the same time, giving seminars and advice to Junior Doctors.

Thanks to **Mr Hekuran Skuqi** the Director of State Reserves, a Government Warehouse was placed at our disposal in the port of Durres. With a firm base to work from Task Force Albania has now begun to stockpile essential items, ready for delivery by the Military to selected Towns and Villages where there is the greatest need.

And so it goes on. Perhaps 1995 will be the year when the **Bosnian** conflict will be resolved and the axe hanging over Albania's head will be lifted. In the meantime, its fragile economy struggles for survival. The investors have come and gone, and sadly – few have returned.

This tiny Balkan Nation desperately needs a lucky break, for it had the courage to shake off the Bonds of Communism that had imprisoned it for almost 50 years. After all that, how ironic its own destiny should lie **"Just out of reach",** and in the hands of others.

Librazsd, April 1995.
To all **Karate-Ka**-

Thank you

Norman Wisdom celebrated his "80th birthday" by going to Albania with John in January 1995. T.F.A. is joining four other British charities in a combined effort to build a medical clinic in Tirana. It will be known as **"The Pitkin Centre"** after Norman's most famous character.

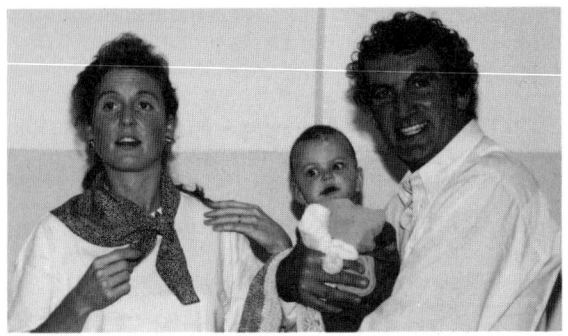

In October 1993, T.F.A. transported aid for **"Her Royal Highness The Duchess of York"** to Tirana's Dystrophic Hospital. Her concern for the malnourished babies was blatantly obvious and within days, she had orchestrated a delivery of essential medicines.

No cure in sight – no place to hide.

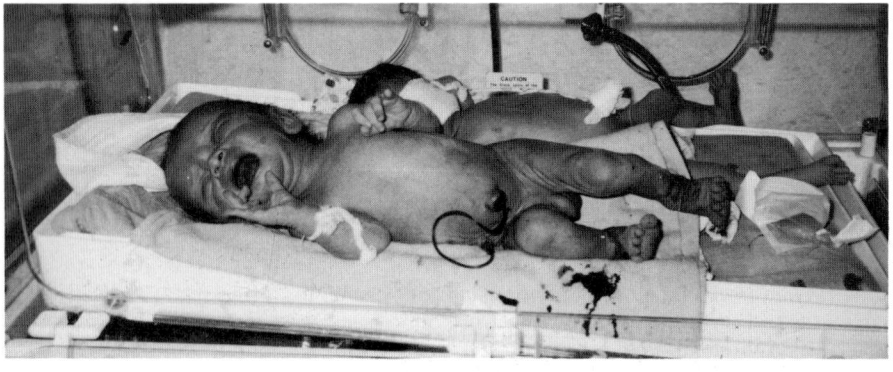

Two babies – one blind – in one incubator, in a maternity hospital without a ventilator.

RECOMMENDED READING

Title:	Karate-Dō Nyūmon
Author:	Gichin Funakoshi
Publisher:	Kodansha International

*Title:	Karate-Dō Kyohan
Author:	Gichin Funakoshi
Publisher:	Kodansha – UK Ward Lock Publications Ltd

*Title:	Karate-Dō: My Way of Life
Author:	Gichin Funakoshi
Publisher:	Kodansha International

Title:	Dynamic Karate
Author:	Masatoshi Nakayama
Publisher:	Ward Lock Publications Ltd

Title:	The Heart of Karate-Dō
Author:	Shigeru Egami
Publisher:	Kodansha International

*Title:	Karate's History and Traditions
Author:	Bruce A. Haines
Publisher:	Charles E. Tuttle & Co

Title:	Diary of the Way
Author:	Ira Lerner
Publisher:	The Ridge Press

Title:	Dynamic Powers of Karate
Author:	Hirokazu Kanazawa
Publisher:	Dragon Books

Title:	Karate – The Art of Empty Hand Fighting
Author:	Hidetaka Nishiyama & Richard C. Brown
Publisher:	Charles E. Tuttle & Co

Title:	Moving Zen
Author:	C. W. Nicol
Publisher:	Willian Morrow & Co. Inc, New York

* Compulsory reading within T.A.S.K. for all attempting black belt rank.

USEFUL NAMES AND ADDRESSES

Martial Arts Commission, 1st Floor, Broadway House, 15-16 Deptford Broadway, London SE8 4PE. Tel: 081-691 3433.
Traditional Association of Shotokan Karate (T.A.S.K.), c/o The Bunyan Centre, Mile Road, Bedford. Tel: (0234) 364481.
All enquiries for membership to T.A.S.K. from individuals or associations should be addressed to: Mr E. McClagish, T.A.S.K. General Secretary at the above address.

IN CONCLUSION

After reading this book, for whatever it is worth, my sincere wish is that it will have contributed in some measure to your knowledge of Shotokan Karate and encouraged you to continue with the study of Karate-Dō.

As a teacher of the art for many years now, I have seen a great number of people come, but alas – a great number of people go. Losing students is terribly disappointing, especially when considering the **tremendous potential** many of them **appear** to have.

First to go is the **"undesirable"**, thankfully eliminating himself, closely followed by many of the **"Instant Kickers"**. Those who have a natural aptitude for the physical accomplishments of Karate but quite early on, find it **"All too easy"** – and give up, without really having ever **tried**. Ultimately, that Western adage would seem to apply – "You can lead a horse to water..."

So who are the people who remain to become the teachers and masters of tomorrow? The answer to that question is, apart from a handful of naturally talented people – **ordinary folk!**

The art of Karate holds a **mystical** appeal for many. Initially perhaps, the ability of a man to put his hand through a brick and later the thought of becoming invincible, repelling any attack by any number of assailants. For the average man to acquire this knowledge and become **"extraordinary"**, is perhaps, in the first instance an enthralling notion and an opportunity too good to miss. Of course, after several months of serious training the student realises he may never become a **"Superman"** and quite probably doesn't want to either. For the idea will be dawning, that the continued practise of basic fundamentals is having an effect on the way he sees, feels and behaves towards other people and at this point, he has begun his journey, along **"The Way"**.

The physical movements of punching, kicking, striking and blocking performed repeatedly, are but a vehicle needed to transport the traveller along "The Way" to his appointed destination. The journey is a gradual one and cannot be undergone in a few months. **There is no substitute for time – and that is what it takes.**

Karate has been described as a **"Moving Zen"** and I personally believe it is akin to religion. It is about helping people, doing someone a good turn – not a bad one and above all, humility. How clear are the words of **"The Dōjō Kun"**, if we can only live up to them.

Unfortunately, we are human, therefore imperfect, but the fact remains – it's not **The Style** that is important but the way in which **The Man** conducts himself and sets an example for others to follow.

Karate-Dō, practised sincerely, will build confidence, promote fitness, improve fighting ability and enhance longevity of life but these are small measure compared to the **"Real"** benefits awaiting you.

GLOSSARY

JAPANESE	PRONUNCIATION	ENGLISH	PAGES
Age Uke	(ah-geh oo-kay)	Rising block	58
Age Zuki	(ah-geh zoo-key)	Rising punch	22
Bassai	(bass-ar-ee)	To penetrate a fortress (formal exercise)	-
Bō	(boh)	Staff	192
Budō	(boo-do. 'o' as in orange)	Martial ways	-
Chinte	(chin-tay)	Chinese hands (formal exercise)	-
Choku Zuki	(cho-koo zoo-key)	Straight punch	14
Chūdan	(chew-dahn)	Middle level	-
Dachi	(dah-chee)	Stance	-
Dan	(dahn)	Level in black belt grade	-
Dō	(dough)	The Way Of	-
Dōjō	(dough-joe)	The Way place/training hall	-
Empi	(en-pee)	Flying swallow (formal exercise)	-
Empi	(en-pee)	Elbow	-
Empi Uchi	(en-pee woo-chee)	Elbow strike	48
Empi Uke	(en-pee oo-kay)	Elbow block	160
Fumikomi	(foo-me-koh-me)	Stamping kick	156
Fudō Dachi	(foo-dough dah-chee)	Immovable stance	11
Gankaku	(gahn-can-koo)	Crane on a rock (formal exercise)	-
Gedan	(geh-dahn)	Lower level	-
Gedan Barai	(geh-dahn baa-rah-ee)	Lower parry	74
Gedan Zuki	(geh-dahn zoo-key)	Lower punch	-
Geri	(geh-rhee)	Kick	78
Gi	(ghee)	Training suit	-
Gohon Kumite	(go-hon ['o' as in orange] koo-me-tay)	5-step sparring	205
Gyaku	(gya-koo)	Reverse	-
Gyaku Zuki	(gya-koo zoo-key)	Reverse punch	18
Hachiji Dachi	(hah-chee-gee dah-chee)	Natural open-leg stance	11
Haishu Uchi	(hi-shoe oo-chee)	Back-hand strike	190
Haishu Uke	(hi-shoe oo-kay)	Back-hand block	190
Haitō	(hi-toe)	Ridge hand	-
Haitō Uchi	(hi-toe oo-chee)	Ridge-hand strike	44
Haitō Uke	(hi-toe oo-kay)	Ridge-hand block	143
Haiwan	(hi-wahn)	Back arm	134
Haiwan Uke	(hi-ee-wahn oo-kay)	Back arm block	-
Hangetsu	(hahn-geh-tsue)	Half moon (formal exercise)	-
Hanmi	(hahn-me)	Half facing position	-
Hara	(hah-rah)	Concept of spiritual centre	7
Hara-Kiri	(hah-rah ki-ree)	Literally: belly cut, slang term for ritual suicide (Seppuku)	-
Heian	(hey-un)	Peaceful mind	-
Heian Shodan	(hey-un sho-['o' as in orange] dahn)	Literally: Peaceful mind 1st level (formal exercise)	117
Heian Nidan	(hey-un knee-dahn)	2nd level	133
Heian Sandan	(hey-un sun-dahn)	3rd level	151
Heian Yondan	(hey-un yon-dahn)	4th level	167
Heian Godan	(hey-un go-dahn)	5th level	185
Heisoku Dachi	(hey-sock-oo dah-chee)	Informal attention stance	169-170
Hidari	(he-dah-rhee)	Left side	-
Hiraken	(he-rah-ken)	Fore-knuckle fist	-
Hiza	(he-zar)	Knee	177-181
Hiza Geri	(he-zar geh-rhee)	Knee kick	181
Hombu	(hom-boo)	Main dojo or HQ	-
Ippon-ken	(eepon-ken)	One-knuckle fist	-
Ippon Nukite	(eepon noo-key-teh)	One-finger spear hand	-
Ji'in	(gee-inn)	Named after Chinese temple 'Jion Ji' (formal exercise)	-
Jion	(gee-on)	Temple (formal exercise)	-
Jitte	(gee-tay)	Ten hands (formal exercise)	-
Jiyū Ippon	(gee-you eepon)	Semi-free one-step	9

JAPANESE	PRONUNCIATION	ENGLISH	PAGES
Kumite	(koo-me-teh)	Sparring	-
Jiyū Kumite	(gee-you koo-me-teh)	Free sparring	-
Jōdan	(joe-dahn)	Upper level	-
Jūji Uke	(jew-gee oo-kay)	'X' block	70
Ka	(kah)	Person or practitioner	-
Kage Uke	(kah-gay oo-kay)	Hooking block	-
Kage Zuki	(kah-gay zoo-key)	Hooking punch	32
Kakato	(kah-kah-toe)	Heel	-
Kakiwake Uke	(kah-key-wah-kay oo-kay)	Wedge block	76
Kamikaze	(kah-me-kah-zay)	Literally: Divine wind. World War II suicide pilots	-
Kankū	(kahn-koo)	To look at the sky	-
Kara	(kah-rah)	Empty – Chinese	-
Kata	(kah-tah)	Formal exercise	99–201
Keage	(kay-ah-geh)	Snap	82
Keitō Uke	(kay-toe oo-kay)	Chicken-head wrist block	98
Kekomi	(kay-koh-me)	Thrust	84
Keri	(kay-rhee)	(geri) Kick	78
Ki	(key)	Inner power – Spirit	-
Kiai	(key-i)	Shout used to unite Ki and Physical	-
Kiba Dachi	(kay-bah dah-chee)	Straddle or horse-riding stance	11
Kihon Ippon Kumite	(key-hone eepone koo-me-teh)	Basic one-step sparring	225
Kime	(key-may)	Focus	-
Kizami Zuki	(key-zah-me zoo-key)	Front snap punch	-
Kin Geri	(as kith and kin geh-rhee)	Groin kick	-
Kokutsu Dachi	(koh-koo-tsue dah-chee)	Back stance	11
Koshi	(ko-shi)	Ball of foot	92
Kumade	(koo-mah-deh)	Bear hand	-
Kumite	(koo-meh-teh)	Sparring	202–288
Kun	(kun. 'u' as 'ou' in 'could'))	Oath	258
Kyu	(quew)	Rank below black belt	-
Ma-ai	(mah-aye)	Distancing	225
Mae	(mah-eh)	Front	-
Mae Geri	(mah-eh geh-rhee)	Front kick	80
Makiwara	(mah-key-wha-rha)	Striking post	-
Mawashi Geri	(mah-wha-she geh-rhee)	Roundhouse kick	86
Mawashi Zuki	(mah-wha-she zoo-key)	Roundhouse punch	24
Mawate	(mah-wha-teh)	Turn	-
Migi	(me-ghee)	Right side	-
Mika Zuki Geri	(me-kah zoo-key geh-rhee)	Crescent kick	90–92
Mizu No Kokoro	(me-zoo-no ko-ko-ro)	Mind like water	185
Mokuso	(mo ['orange'] koo-so ['orange'])	Meditation	-
Morote Uke	(moe-row-teh oo-kay)	Augmented block	64
Morote Zuki	(moe-row-teh zoo-key)	Augmented punch	20
Nagashi Uke	(nah-gah-she oo-kay)	Stepping block	-
Naha-te	(nah-hah-tay)	Okinawan school of karate	-
Nakadaka-Ippon-Ken	(nar-kah-dah-kar eepone-ken)	Middle-finger one-knuckle fist	-
Nami-Ashi	(nah-mee ah-she)	Inside leg block	-
Neko Ashi Dachi	(neh-koh ah-she dah-she)	Cat stance	11
Nidan Geri	(nee-dahn geh-rhee)	Double kick	-
Nihon Nukite	(nee-hone noo-key-teh)	Two-finger spear hand	-
Nukite	(noo-key-teh)	Spear hand straight thrust	137
Obi	(o ['orange']-bee)	Belt-sash	-
Oi Zuki	(oh-ee zoo-key)	Stepping punch	16
Okinawa-te	(o-kin-ar-wah-teh)	Okinawan school of karate	-
Rei	(ray)	Bow	-
Ren Zuki	(wren zoo-key)	Alternate punching	174
Ryu	(ree-you)	School (of karate)	275
Sambon Kumite	(sam-bon ['orange'] koo-me-tey)	3-step sparring	219
Seiken	(say-ken)	Forefist	12
Seiza	(say-zar)	Kneeling position (meditation posture)	-
Sempai	(sem-pie)	Senior	-
Sensei	(sen-say)	Teacher	-

JAPANESE	PRONUNCIATION	ENGLISH	PAGES
Seppuku	(sep-poo-koo)	Ritual suicide	-
Shihan	(she-hahn)	Master (6th dan and above)	-
Shiro	(she-roe)	White	-
Shizentai	(she-zen-tah-ee)	Natural stance	-
Shutō	(shoe-toe)	Knife hand	36
Shutō Uchi	(shoe-toe oo-chee)	Knife-hand strike	36–37
Shutō Uke	(shoe-toe oo-kay)	Knife-hand block	66
Sochin	(saw-chin)	Takes name from Immovable stance (formal exercise)	-
Sokutō	(sow-koo-toe)	Foot edge	82–84
Soto Ude Uke	(so-toh oo-day oo-kay)	Outside forearm block	60
Taikyoku	(tar-eek-yo-koo)	First cause	-
Taikyoku Shodan	(tar-eek-yo-koo sho-dahn)	First cause (formal exercise)	101
Tai Sabaki	(tar-ee sah-bah-kee)	Body shifting	-
T.A.S.K.		Traditional Association of Shotokan Karate	327
Tate Shutō Uke	(tah-teh shoe-toe oo-kay)	Vertical knife-hand block	68
Te	(teh)	Hand	-
Teishō	(tay-sho)	Palm heel	-
Teishō Uchi	(tay-sho oo-chee)	Palm-heel strike	-
Teishō Uke	(tay-sho oo-kay)	Palm-heel block	172
Tekki Nidan*	(teh-key knee-dahn)	2nd level	-
Tekki Sandan*	(teh-key sahn-dahn)	3rd level	-
Tekki Shodan*	(teh-key sho-dahn)	1st level	-
Tettsui	(tett-sooie)	Bottom fist	-
Tettsui Uchi	(tett-sooie oo-chee)	Bottom-fist strike	40
Tobi	(tow-be)	Jumping	-
Tsuki	(tsue-key)	Punching	12
Uchi	(oo-chee)	Strike	34
Uchi Ude Uke	(oo-chee oo-day oo-kay)	Inside block (forearm)	62
Ude	(oo-day)	Forearm	-
Uke	(oo-kay)	Block	56
Unsu	(oon-soo)	Hands of the cloud (formal exercise)	-
Ura Zuki	(oo-rah zoo-key)	Close punch	26
Uraken	(oo-rah ken)	Back fist	42
Ushiro Empi	(oo-she-row en-pee)	Reverse elbow	-
Ushiro Geri	(oo-she-row geh-rhee)	Back kick	88
Ushiro Mawashi Geri	(oo-she-row mah-wha-she geh-rhee)	Back roundhouse kick	94
Washide	(wah-she-deh)	Eagle hand (beak)	-
Wankan	(wahn-kahn)	Shortest shotokan formal exercise	-
Yama Zuki	(yah-mah zoo-key)	'U' punch	30
Yame	(yah-may)	Stop – finish	-
Yoi	(as in 'boy')	Ready	-
Yoko	(yoh-koh)	Side	-
Yoko Empi Uchi	(yoh-koh en-pee oo-chee)	Side elbow strike	52
Yoko Geri	(yoh-koh geh-rhee)	Side kick	82–84
Zazen	(zar-zen)	Seated meditation	-
Zen	(zen)	Form of Buddhism based on meditation	-
Zenkutsu Dachi	(zen-koo-tsue dah-chee)	Front stance	-
Zuki	(zoo-key)	Punch	12

*Tekki means horse riding. These 3 formal exercises take their name from the Straddle stance (Kiba Dachi)